Return to Belgium

The true story of four brave women parachuted into Belgium to help the Resistance before liberation.

Copyright © 2009 Bernard O'Connor

All rights reserved.

Attempts have been made to locate, contact and acknowledge copyright holders of quotes and illustrations used in my work. They have been credited within the text and/or in the bibliography. Much appreciation is given to those who have agreed that I include their work. Any copyright owners who are not properly identified and acknowledged, get in touch so that I may make any necessary corrections.

Small parts of this book may be reproduced in similar academic works providing due acknowledgement is given in the introduction and within the text. Any errors or suggested additions can be forwarded to me for future editions.

Bernard O'Connor

Visit my website at
http://www.bernardoconnor.org.uk

ISBN 978-1-902810-35-X

Introduction

The Comète Escape Line: Belgium to France to Spain to Britain

SOE and the Belgian Country Section

Elaine Madden

Denise Leplat

The anonymous Belgian blonde

Olga Jackson

Madeleine Fouconnier

Frédérique Dupuich

Bibliography

Bernard O'Connor

INTRODUCTION

When I moved to the small village of Everton in Bedfordshire, UK, in the summer of 1992 I endeavoured to research its history. I was told by regulars in the Thornton Arms public house that the airfield at the bottom of the Greensand Ridge, where I walked my West Highland Terrier, was used during the Second World War. An old gentleman who lived in the village was said to have worked there, so I called on him to enquire about life on the airfield during the war. He refused, arguing that he had signed the Official Secrets Act. This was a government order to all those who were involved in secret operations. Other locals I spoke to knew it was used during the war but not what for. As I discovered; they were not meant to know. Many of the official documents I found that mentioned the airfield were stamped MOST SECRET.

Trying to find out what went on there so many years ago has been rather like doing a jigsaw puzzle but it as if the box has been tipped out and the pieces scattered to the four winds. Over the years I have found lots of the pieces, by no means all, but enough to be able to recreate a good picture of what was on the lid. Some pieces fitted together perfectly. Others had all or parts of the edges worn off, so I am unsure if where I have put them is right. As the majority of the pieces date back many decades, some have a rather faded picture but still look like they fit. There are gaps in this account, some large but, the more I have worked on it, the more I have realised that I have been trying to reassemble several jigsaw puzzles.

After publishing a booklet, *'Tempsford Airfield: Now the Story can be Told'* in 1997, I have had to update it regularly as more information has come to light. In short, it was from this airfield that supplies and agents were sent to help the resistance in occupied Europe. The present edition has had to be renamed *'RAF Tempsford, Churchill's MOST SECRET airfield during World War*

Two'. Whilst researching its history, I discovered that over sixty women were infiltrated as couriers, wireless operators, sabotage instructors and, in some cases, organisers. The vast majority were parachuted in or landed by boat or plane in France; three were parachuted into Holland and four into Belgium.

Researching the Internet, reading books, journals and newspapers on this period, communicating with people and accessing documents in museums and in the National Archives, I have uncovered a story, parts of which may be known to some, that sheds light on the work of the British Special Operations Executive (SOE), the Secret Intelligence Service (SIS), the American Office of Strategic Services (OSS) and the Belgian Sûreté de l'Etat in their efforts to expel the German armies from occupied Europe. It also tells a story of several remarkable women who played an active part in liberating their country.

After Hitler's armed forces were successful in taking over Czechoslovakia and Poland in 1939 and invading Denmark and Norway in April 1940, on 10 May, he ordered the *Sichelschnitt,* an armed attack on France, Luxembourg, Belgium and the Netherlands. It was the Whitsun weekend when almost everyone was on holiday. Because of the extensive preparations that Belgium had made in the 1930s to prevent an invasion, it was arguably the best prepared country in Europe to defend itself against the Axis forces at the start of World War Two. However, as King Léopold III had not made an alliance with the French or the British, he was unable to coordinate effectively with the British Expeditionary Force or the French Army.

The speed and ferocity of German Panzer divisions in their push to the Channel ports caught the Belgian armed forces off-guard. Paratroopers rained down onto Belgian soil and Stuka planes dive-bombed important transport links. The Allied forces in the country ordered a retreat, blowing up bridges as they left. During this *Blitzkrieg* nearly a quarter of Belgium's approximately nine million inhabitants fled. Its troop movements were impeded by escaping motorists and an increased sense of panic arose when those governing, managerial and administrative classes with money went to stay with relatives or friends in the country, or, if they had cars, much further away to what they thought was freedom. About two million people drove into France, some settling in the Pyrenees, close to the Spanish border. Others managed to get overseas, including Britain..

Hitler's plans included utilising Belgium's airfields from where the Luftwaffe could attack Britain, then use their factories for his war effort and transport able-bodied Belgian men to work in Germany's factories whilst their men were in the Wehrmacht. It was also vital to secure transport routes across northwest Europe, particularly the Atlantic and North Sea ports.

Holland, as the British and Americans called the country during the Second World War, surrendered on 15 May, two days after their royal family and government had been shipped to safety in England. Their motoring population could not escape though Belgium. The Germans pushed through to the coast within days. The Belgian artillery managed to hold off the full force of the Blitzkrieg for eighteen days, enough time to allow the start of a major evacuation of over three hundred thousand British, Canadian, Belgian and French soldiers and civilians from the beaches at Dunkirk.

How many amongst those who managed to escape over the next nine days were women is impossible to say, but there were said to be about 1,300 French Nursing sisters. I have discovered that amongst the others was Elaine Madden, a 17-year old Belgium girl. But she was different. Dressed in soldiers' clothes, she had joined the British Expeditionary Force in its attempt to escape the advancing German troops, arriving in England on 30 May 1940. Almost four years later, she was one of four women who agreed to be infiltrated back into Belgium, just weeks before its liberation.

Something like 40,000 Allied troops did not get into any of the 850 boats that crossed the Channel. They were either defending the main body of troops on the beach or were too sick or wounded. Eight to ten thousand of these troops surrendered in June 1940 at St Valery-en-Caux and, for some, it was the end of the war. For others, who did not want to spend years in a prisoner-of-war camp, they followed the military directive to take whatever means they could to escape and rejoin their units or try to make their way back to Britain. That meant risking their lives but there were well over a thousand civilians who equally risked their and their families' lives to try and get these people out of Belgium, across France and into neutral Switzerland or Spain. The story of one of these, Andrée De Jongh, has been told elsewhere but her role in this account needs to be emphasised.

One woman, Frédérique Dupuich, accompanied Andrée with a group of nine Belgians over the Pyrenees in 1941, eventually reached England and, after a few years, agreed to return, this time by parachute. The third, Olga Thioux, later Olga Jackson, was a British woman who had lived in Belgium before the war broke out, but who also volunteered to be parachuted back in. The fourth, understandably anonymous, was a young woman whose husband had been arrested as a member of the Belgian resistance and executed. She escaped to England and agreed to return on a particularly sensitive mission. When she was sent back remains a mystery but the other three jumped in the early hours of the morning on two consecutive nights at the beginning of August 1944. What their missions were and how successful they were, I have tried to found out.

This period of Belgium's history has been exhaustively covered by military historians and the role played by the secret services of both countries has been detailed in Michael Foot's *The SOE in the Low Countries'.* My work explores the lives of some of the women involved and identifies their links with RAF Tempsford.

In order to tell the story of these remarkable women and others involved in the Belgian resistance, I would like to acknowledge the assistance of the staff at the National Archives in Kew, John Clinch, Philippe Connart, Rien Emmery, Anne Griffin, Steven Kippax,

Return to Belgium

Adeline Remy, Lieven Saerens, Xavier Van Tilborg and the following websites: 64-Baker Street, belgiumww2, Comète line, comete-bidassoa, 91stbombgroup, dbnl (bibliotheek voor de Nederlandse letteren), historylearningsite, Spartacus, the specialoperationsexecutive user group on yahoo.com and Wikipedia.

The Comète Escape Line: Belgium to France to Spain to Britain

One of the Belgians attributed after the war with setting up one of the numerous escape lines for those who had not managed to get out of Dunkirk was 24-year-old Andrée De Jongh. Whilst she was not parachuted into Belgium, she played a vital role in the resistance and her story helps provide the background to the other women.

Known to her fiends as Dedée, she was involved in the establishment of what has become known as the Comète Escape Line. She chose to carry on the work of two fellow resistance workers who had been captured by the Germans within months of escorting the first Allied servicemen out of Belgium.

Andrée grew up, a schoolmaster's daughter, in the family house at No. 73 Avenue Emile Verhaeren in the suburb of Schaerbeek, Brussels. As a teenager, she studied graphic design and, before the war, helped her brother-in-law get his Jewish friend out of Nazi Germany.

As an indication as to what sort of a girl she was like growing up, her father's pet name for her was 'Little Cyclone'. As a child, one of her heroines was Edith Cavell, the British nurse shot in Brussels in 1915 for helping about 200 First World War troops escape from Belgium into Holland. This was a network run by Philippe Baucq, hence known subsequently as the Baucq-Cavell line. The other was Gabrielle Petit, a Red Cross nurse, who, when her soldier fiancé was wounded, helped him escape over the border into Holland where he was able to rejoin his regiment. There, she used her photographic memory to supply British Intelligence with valuable information about German troop deployment. Persuaded to work for the British, she was sent to England for training and re-entered Belgium as a special agent, distributing *La Libre Belgique,* a clandestine paper. Betrayed and captured in February 1916, she refused to beg for clemency before a firing squad on 1 April. Scorning a blindfold, she cried out 'Now you will see how a Belgium woman can die.' (Rafferty, J.' The Last of the

Line, undated article from John Prost Newspaper Collection in the Lincolnshire Aviation Heritage Escape Room)

Andrée's father used to read stories to her about these two brave women and the visits she paid to Gabrielle's memorial prompted her to train as a nurse. Surviving the Second World War, in an interview with Shirin Wheeler for the *Bulletin,* a Brussels English Language weekly magazine, she admitted that when King Léopold, the Commander-in-chief of the Army, surrendered on 27 May,

> *I'd never seen my father cry before - never. He said: listen Belgium isn't fighting anymore. It's given up. I was in despair and furious, enraged at the same time. I said to my father, 'You are wrong to cry. You'll see what we'll do to them. You'll see, they are going to lose this war. They've started it, but they'll lose it. Don't worry." But I really didn't have any idea how we would win.* (http://home.clara.net/clinchy/bulletin.htm 18 May 2009)

Maybe, as Commander-in-Chief of the Belgian Army, King Leopold felt he would save hundreds of thousands of his people from being slaughtered. Within days, the territories of Eupen, Malmédy and St. Vith had been annexed to the German Reich and the rest of Belgium occupied. The decision caused a royal furore. Many in his civil government, who had retreated to Limoges, condemned the surrender, arguing that it ought to have been a political decision. The king stayed under house arrest at the Royal Palace at Laeken in Brussels whilst the population was left to face the victorious invaders. Initially, the government fled to Paris and, following the fall of France in June 1940, to Vichy. Some fled to Bordeaux from where four top ministers escaped to London, accusing the King of treason.

Andrée's philosophy in all this was simple. In an interview reported in her obituary in the *Daily Telegraph* in 2007, she said that she knew what needed to be done when war was declared. "*There was no hesitation. We could not stop what we had to do although we knew the cost. Even if it was at the expense of our lives, we had to fight until the last breath.*"

In Rafferty's article, 'The Last of the Line', she commented that

I was very indignant and angry against the Germans …I thought we must not accept this. We are a small neutral country but we are neutral and they have signed this. They pass through the country and they kill people and not taking any notice of what they have signed. I already thought this matter about the Jewish people was a scandal. I thought, this is really a shame for those people to put all the faults on them, just because they are Jewish. This is quite crazy. For all those reasons I was very annoyed about them. I was so deeply motivated it was rare when I was afraid. (Rafferty, op.cit.)

There were many Belgians like her, men and women who wanted to continue fighting, in whatever way they could. Andrée was working as a commercial artist for the Sofina company in Malmédy when war broke out. She returned immediately to Brussels, where she volunteered to work with the Red Cross and look after the large numbers of people being brought into the military hospital at Saint-Jean-de-Bruges for emergency treatment.

After the battle of St Valery-en-Caux, where French troops surrendered to Rommel on 11 June 1940 and the British 51st (Highland) Infantry Division on the 12th, the conscript-heroes.com website stated that:

… the Germans began bringing thousands of British prisoners of war captured at St Valery-en-Caux. These soldiers were made to march many miles per day on their way to the trains and barges that were to take them to prisoner of war camps in the east of the German Reich. The prisoners were lightly guarded and escape was relatively easy, so by the time the columns of prisoners reached Belgium,

dozens of them were slipping away and finding shelter with sympathetic villagers and farmers. There, many of the soldiers stayed, through the summer and autumn, well fed and cared for, but with no obvious route home. (http://www.conscript-heroes.com/escapelines/EscapeLines.html 17 June 2009)

Andrée's boss, Baron Jacques Donny, was one of a number of figures working behind the scenes, financing those who had evaded capture or escaped, providing them with food, shelter, civilian clothes and false papers. Andrée helped with these tasks as well as finding some of them safe houses in and around Brussels and encouraging her friends to help. Using her First Aid training, she helped to nurse the injured, many of whom were desperate to return to their families and fight to protect them from the forces amassing on the Channel coast in preparation for an invasion. There was an urgency to get them to Britain to fight again and plans had to be made to provide them with safe passage out of the country.

During the Second World War, the circumstances for exfiltrating people were much harder than in the First. Holland had been overrun, while the whole of France was under direct or indirect Nazi control, divided between a German-occupied zone in the north and a collaborationist Vichy zone in the south. The Atlantic coast had an exclusion zone imposed along its length and a line of defences known as the Atlantik Wall started to be constructed. Getting people out by sea was virtually impossible. According to Andrée's obituary in *The Times,*

She spent a year studying the many German regulations about control of movement, helping wounded Allied soldiers in Belgian hospitals to send letters home through the Red Cross and sounding out close friends about setting up an escape organisation. She had worse to wrestle with than Miss Cavell, who had only to move men across the Dutch frontier. This time the Netherlands were also occupied, as were Luxembourg and northern and western France; Alsace and Lorraine had been re-annexed into Germany and south-eastern France, governed from Vichy, seemed to her a satellite of the Nazi Reich. (http://www.timesonline.co.uk/tol/comment/obituaries/article2657876.ece)

Baron Jacques Donny was not the only member of the Belgian aristocracy concerned about what had happened to their country. According to the Comète line website, some time in July 1940, Gérard Waucquez, a Brussels industrialist, was entrusted with a message to deliver to Viscount Davignon, the Belgian ambassador in Berlin. The message contained the conditions of surrender of the Belgian army in France. Waucquez was the nephew of Hubert Pierlot, the Belgian Prime minister who was in exile in Britain and also a family friend of Baron Goffinet, the aide de camp of Prince Charles, the Count of Flanders and King Léopold's brother, who was in hiding in Brussels for fear of being captured by the Germans. On 2 September 1940, Princess Marie de Ligne, asked Waucquez for help in arranging the evacuation of a Captain Woolton, the grandson of Field Marshal Douglas Haig, Britain's Commander in Chief during the Somme offensive. Waucquez volunteered.

He and Woolton caught the bus to Paris, reached Bayonne by train and Saint-Jean-de-Luz by bicycle. There they met Mr. Willems, a Belgian refugee, with a Mr. Arajama, the chief of a band of Spanish Republican refugees who were running a smuggling business. The cost of getting an evader over the border into Spain in 1940 was £40 for an officer and £20 for other ranks. Prices rose dramatically as the war progressed with eventually gold sovereigns being needed.

After leaving Hendaye, they swam across the River Bidassoa, a raging torrent after heavy rain or snowmelt and then scrambled up the opposite bank to Irun. From there, Arajama took them to the British Consul in Bilbao where Waucquez met a Mr. Dean who worked at the consulate in Marseilles. Waucquez then met his uncle and Paul Spaak, his Foreign Minister, who were under house arrest in Spain. They gave him a document to be forwarded to Camille Gutt, the Minister of Economic Affairs, and August de Vleeschauwer, the Minister for Colonies, who were already in London. The document provided information on the German naval concentrations in Antwerp, Terneuzen, Vlissingen, Ostend and Dunkirk and their plans for the manufacture of ammunition and armoured turrets. Having passed this message on to the British consulate, Waucquez had completed his diplomatic mission and was back in Belgium by 25 September 1940. His experience was to stand him in good stead.

By the end of that year, Andrée was also doing courier work, carrying messages between various members of the Belgian resistance. In early 1941, she was working with 32-year-old Arnold Deppé, a film technician. Before being called up in 1939, he had been working for Gaumont, the French film company, in southwest France. Although arrested after Dunkirk, he escaped from a prisoner-of-war camp near Essen and got back to Brussels where he stayed with his cousin, Henri de Bliqui, a town council employee. Their group became known as 'Equipe DDD' (de Bliqui, Deppé and De Jongh). After de Bliqui was arrested in his home in April 1941 in what was called the "Affair Victor Moreau", Deppé was questioned by the *Geheime Feldpolizei* (GFP), but managed to avoid imprisonment. When he was released, he managed to get away to Brest in Brittany and lie low for a month. Whilst there he found out that a number of evaders and their couriers had been caught and held in concentration camps in Vichy France.

When Deppé returned to Brussels in May 1941, he helped a French doctor, Mr. Kampf, and a British captain, Jeffrey Collins, who had made an unsuccessful attempt to escape over the Pyrenees. They realised that a much more secure line had to be planned. They discussed establishing an escape line to get Belgian volunteers aiming at joining the government-in-exile in London and any airmen or soldiers of the Expeditionary Force who had been left behind. Their presence was becoming extremely expensive and hazardous.

In June 1941, Deppé went by train to the Basques region in the south-western Pyrenees, escorting two escaped French prisoners. As he had worked in Aquitaine between 1929 and 1939 and had lived in Saint Jean-de-Luz, close to the Spanish border, he knew the area well. Eventually he found Alejandro Lizade, who organised a group of 'passeurs', guides who knew the goat and sheep tracks over the mountains like the back of their hands. For a few thousand French francs a head, they were willing to guide evaders over the border into neutral Spain.

Deppé had been given the address and password, "Gogo est mort", for Madame Elvire De Greef, who had moved from the Brussels suburb of Etterbeek with her husband and family to 'safety' in the small town of Anglet between Biarritz and Bayonne. She was already involved in helping Allied soldiers get into Spain using Alejanadro Elizalde's team of smugglers. Known later as *Tante Go*, she agreed to find safe houses between Bayonne and Hendaye where 'visitors' could stay until the '*passeur*' thought there were suitable weather conditions for the crossing. To assist even more, her husband stole passes from the local Kommandantur in Anglet, where he worked as a translator for the German occupying forces.

According to the Comète Line poster in the Lincolnshire Aviation Heritage Centre, escapees were hidden in safe houses in Biarritz and Cibour. Travel clothes were exchanged for very old clothes and their shoes for espadrilles, rope-soled sandals that were far better for climbing over the mountains, quieter and with a better grip. Their clothes and shoes were returned to Paris for re-use. Depending on the route taken, the weather conditions and German and Spanish patrols, it used to take between one and five days. Reaching either Irun or Pamplona, the escapees would be taken to the British Consul in San Sebastian.

During the June trip, Deppé had arranged a crossing of the River Somme near Corbie, east of Amiens, and made arrangements for a safe house with his aunt in Paris and good friends in Lille. Then, on 12 July 1941, he and Andrée accompanied a group of ten Belgians over the border into Spain in an attempt to reach London. On the Comète line blogspot it names one of them as a "Miss Richards" but I have found out that this was an alias. Her real name was Frédérique Dupuich. Who she was and exactly what she was doing with the men is now known; she was a secret agent on the run and was one of the first to travel the length of what became known affectionately by the successful evaders as 'Line DD' and then later as the Comète Line.

Generally, those who succeeded in crossing into Spain were directed to Lisbon if they were civilians and Gibraltar if they were in the Armed Forces. In both cases, stringent checks were undertaken to ensure that they were bona fide refugees and not a German spy. They were also questioned at length by MI9 about the routes they had taken and the names and addresses of those who had helped them. This was vital intelligence as MI9, otherwise known as I.S.9.d., was organising and funding the escape lines. Its headquarters was in Room 900 at the War Office in London but it had offices in Lisbon and Gibraltar. As the cost of training RAF pilots was about £10,000, it was felt worthwhile to spend a little more to get them and their aircrews back to Britain as it was cheaper than training new airmen.

Philippe Connart, an authority on the Comète Line, provided me with some details about Frédérique. There had been no mention of her in any of the literature I had read relating to the work of the Special Operations Executive (SOE) and the Secret Intelligence Service (SIS), top secret British organisations who were supporting the resistance movements in occupied Europe. Their roles will be become clearer later.

Born in January 1900, Frédérique took up English nationality after the war but, during the 1930s, she worked as a company secretary in Brussels. In

September 1940, four months after the German occupation, she decided to join a Belgian underground movement gathering military and industrial intelligence north and west of Brussels for Walthere Déwé, codenamed 'Clarence'. On 20 June 1940, he established a network made up of veterans of *La Dame Blanche,* an underground group which had operated during the First World War. (Jeffrey, K. *MI6: The History of the Secret Intelligence Service 1909 -1909*, Bloomsbury, London, pp.388 - 389) Exactly what work she did for them is unknown.

According to the 'Belgian 1914-1918' and the 'praats' websites, Déwé had supplied information about the build up of German activity near the border. However, his work was limited by not having wireless receivers. Various attempts were made to get typed documents to London but when escape by sea became increasingly difficult, the time it took for agents to get through France, Switzerland or Spain and back to England meant that the information was often out-of-date by the time it reached London.

He contacted an SIS agent, codenamed *Daniel*, with the offer of providing the British with military and economic intelligence. In response, he was supplied with four telegraph transmitters which were set up in Liège, Brussels, Namur and Marche. Messages were then sent to Major Page, the SIS liaison officer with the Sûreté de l'Etat in London. Intelligence was then passed on through Mr Lepage to the Belgian government, the Belgian and French Armies and King Leopold III. Long before the invasion in May 1940.

It was not until 12/13 January 1941 that Jean Lamy was parachuted by a 138 Squadron pilot from Newmarket racecourse into the Ardennes. One of the other parachutes accompanying him carried a more sophisticated radio transmitter as well as a receiver. However, lax security meant he was caught transmitting on 26 March. Luckily, he had time to destroy the set and his code book before being arrested but underwent months of interrogation before being sentenced to death in January 1942. He spent three years in concentration camps but died from his ill-treatment in 1945.

The work had to go on and *Clarence* produced a weekly report, which, every six weeks, was transported in a tiny box by *Aristide,* one of their agents, to Vichy France and, via the United States embassy in Switzerland, on to London.

Transmissions to Page did not stop but, over time, a number of sets were detected by the Abwehr's radio-goniometry vans. Three vans and occasionally men carrying detection equipment, listened for the wireless transmissions and took compass bearings. Once three bearings had been taken and plotted onto a map, where the lines intersected became their target. Wielding sledgehammers and taking guns and Alsatian dogs, a team would search the property from cellar to attic, arresting anyone suspected of involvement in what had been made an illegal activity. Being in possession of a wireless set and listening to the BBC's Belgian service was an imprisonable offence. Transmitting was tantamount to treason.

In May 1941, an urgent meeting was held in the house of Henriette Dupuich, 25 rue Edmond Picard in Brussels, where *Veramme* had a transmitter. Whether Henriette was Frédérique's mother, sister, aunt or unrelated remains unknown but the surname can hardly be a coincidence. *Saturne*, another member of the *Clarence* network, was suspicious when they noticed several vehicles stopped in front of the house next door. Even though the danger was extreme, he was able to telephone Henriette and warn *Varamme* to hide the set and make himself scarce.

In July 1941, following the betrayal and arrest of one of her friends in her network, Frédérique decided it was time to get out. As being interned for the duration of the war was not what she wanted, she made herself known to 'Ligne DD', run by Deppé and Andrée. They helped her to travel through France using the name 'Miss Richards'. According to her obituary in the *Dorset Evening Echo*,

Once they reached the small town of La Corbie near Amiens, on the banks of the River Somme, which formed a line known as Zone Interdite or Prohibited Zone (the Red Line, the border of what the Germans called *Belgien und Nordfrankreick Bezirk,) they had to find a way of crossing the Somme, without being detected, as it was regularly patrolled by the enemy. Most of the men and Miss Richards couldn't swim and therefore, the inner tube of a large tyre was used with Andrée having to make several return trips pushing them across before they could rest and sleep in the farmhouse of a women nicknamed Nénette (*Renée Boulanger) *in the village of Hamelet on the opposite side of the Somme. 'Next time', Andrée thought, 'we will need the use of a boat.' The following morning the party made their way to Paris and then by the overnight train to Biarritz and the home of Madame Elvire De Greef. A Basque guide was then employed to guide them over the Pyrenees, and to the Spanish side of the border, where they were left to make their own way to San Sebastian. The journey had been a success, or so it was thought until Andrée and Arnold returned to Anglet and learnt that their party had been arrested in Spain and taken back to the border and handed over to the Germans. 'Next time', Andrée said, 'evaders must be taken direct to the British Consulate in Bilbao.'* (Undated obituary in Dorset Evening Echo)

Andrée had utilised the services of Florentino Goicoechea, a Basque *passeur*, to guide the group over the border. According to Airey Neave, the head of MI9, Florentino had

> "fabulous knowledge of the mountains. He was able to find his way in all weathers, even under the influence of cognac. He could always scent danger. When there was fog, which hid every landmark, he could still find

the path. He would stop for a moment and tap the ground with his espadrilles. Then, finding the way, he would move off at a great pace, with the party stumbling and slipping behind him. it was useless to ask him to go more slowly. Often, on the blackest of nights, he could find a single tree trunk or a rock. He would search rapidly, and bring out a spare pair of espadrilles or a bottle of cognac which he had hidden months before. His French vocabulary was limited to 'doucement, doucement' and 'tais toi'". (Neave, A. (1969), *Saturday at MI9,* Hodder and Staughton)

Neave had been the first British officer to escape from Colditz Castle, cross both the Alps and Pyrenees and get back to England, His experiences made him an ideal candidate for MI9, working behind the scenes to help Allied aircrews and others get back to Britain. There were numerous difficulties though.

General Franco, the military leader of nationalist Spain, had a pro-Nazi foreign policy and any captured evaders were incarcerated at prisons like Miranda de Ebro, about 120 kilometres southwest of Bilbao. Once the British consul had been informed of their presence, an attempt was made to get them out. This normally involved paying a large fine for them entering the country illegally. On one occasion, Spanish soldiers who had caught Andrée, were taking her to the authorities for questioning when they stopped at a café. She used the opportunity to slip a note to the proprietor asking him to send it to the Belgian consul. She thought it was his intervention that allowed her out of prison after ten days in captivity. From there, she made her way over the Mediterranean to Tangier, Morocco, where her sister lived, and later, back across to Gibraltar.

Only two of the evaders were reported on Christopher Long's website on the Royal Air Force Escaping Society as getting back to England. Connart says that two managed to get back to Belgium. An officer called Rousseau was arrested in Biarritz and the seven others, including Frédérique, eventually reached London. She arrived in England on 10 September 1941 and, after being interrogated at the Royal Victoria Patriotic School in Wandsworth, south London, to determine whether or not she was an enemy agent. She quickly gained employment at the office of the section head of the London-based Political Warfare Executive (PWE) and the Propaganda Department of the Belgium Sûreté de l'Etat. This was their security service in exile, which was in rivalry with the *Deuxième Section*, the intelligence branch of the exiled general staff. Their problems were mirrored in the British SOE and SIS and their dealings with the War Office.

Documents relating to Frédérique's application for British naturalisation after the war showed that from 17 October 1941 until 7 June 1943 she had a room in the De Vere Hotel in London, W.8 after which she lodged with Dorothy Levers, a friend of her mother, at 17 Thornton Street, also in W.8. (The National Archives (TNA) HO 405/10578) Whilst at work she must have got to know Airey Neave who had been taken on by MI9 as an intelligence officer. He and Jimmy Langley had an office in Room 900 in the War Office with the task of funding and supplying the escape lines getting people out of occupied Europe. In his book, *Little Cyclone,* Langley described Frédérique as '*the plump lady with the panama hat*'. As we shall see, she was to play an important role towards the end of war when she was landed in northern France on a top secret mission back in Belgium.

When Arnold Deppé was arrested by the Gestapo in Lille on 19 August 1941, Andrée was lucky. She had been travelling on a different train. Victor Demets, a Belgian double agent, had infiltrated their network and betrayed them to the Gestapo. Huge rewards, sometimes up to a million francs, were offered for information leading to the arrest of what the Germans called 'terrorists'. Some people succumbed. These *V-Manner,* could make a good living turning people in.

Deppé was held in secret custody in Lille prison and then put in a cell at Saint Gilles until January 1942. Tortured without results, he was sentenced to death and imprisoned at Rheinbach, Mauthausen, Natzweiler-Struthof and Dachau from where he was liberated by the Americans in May 1945.

With both Bliqui and Deppé arrested and her parents being questioned about her whereabouts, it was too dangerous for Andrée to return home. Instead, she moved her operations to a safe house in Valenciennes, where Charles Morelle, a French officer who she and Deppé had helped escape in June, was staying. Although her parents did not know exactly what she was doing, they were able to guess. She was convinced that the Gestapo had also infiltrated some French resistance groups so was very concerned about security.

When she got a message through to her father, whom she knew she could trust, he agreed to run the Belgian side of the operation. Without any training in clandestine operations, she still felt able to continue, probably because she knew that single men or groups of men were more likely to be stopped and questioned than women or couples.

Accompanying her on her next trip on 19 August 1941 were two Belgian volunteers, Robert Merchiers and Ernest Sterckmans, and James Cromar, a private in the 1st Scottish Highland Regiment. The Comète line website indicates that Robert Merchiers was an early resistant who had been arrested and released by chance and that Ernest Sterckmans belonged to one of the families offering safe houses to evaders. Researching this escape, I found a link with Elaine Madden, the young girl who was evacuated from Dunkirk dressed as a soldier. The Comète line website stated that between winter 1940 and spring 1941, Robert Goffinet had given a lot of valuable information and funds to Waucquez. It was specifically to help feed and shelter clandestine British soldiers. Later in the war, in August 1944, Elaine was secretly parachuted into Belgium as a courier. Part of her mission was to assist in getting Prince Charles out of the country and back to Britain.

To commemorate the first anniversary of the invasion, Goffinet invited Waucquez to bring two evaders, downed RAF pilot Sergeant Leonard Warburton and James Cromar, round to his house for dinner. Each was given five gold guineas to help them get back to Britain. Once Andrée got them into Spain, she conveyed them personally to the British consulate in Bilbao. In an interview after the war with Shirin Wheeler, a BBC journalist, she admitted that,

> "I have really awful memories of that. All those men, they were our children, it's true. We were so attached to them. In fact we still are. As soon as we spotted the car, there was no time to say goodbye. They ran. We had spent three days together - we couldn't even say goodbye. My heart would melt, but at the same time I was so happy." (http://home.clara.net/clinchy/bulletin.htm, 18 May 2009)

Colonel Dansey and Captain James Langley, MI9 officers in London, were reported to have been suspicious of Andrée at first but the consulate eventually persuaded them that her radiant integrity could not be forged. In her obituary in the *Daily Telegraph* it stated that the vice-consul was initially sceptical, thinking that it might be a German plot to infiltrate their agents in the guise of Belgian evaders. He could hardly believe that so petite and attractive a young girl could have walked over the mountains following a smugglers' trail after travelling across occupied France. He told her he would have to refer her plan to the British embassy in Madrid. Her response was that she would be back in a few weeks with more men.

Airey Neave, the co-ordinator of the London-based escape and evasion organisation at MI9, was alerted to the appearance of this intriguing girl. A flow of telegrams and reports ensued as attempts were made to establish her authenticity.

Donald Darling, MI9's representative in the Bilbao consulate, recalled telling her that, if she was to return with bona fide RAF personnel, she would be given the funds she had requested to cover her expenses. This money could be used to buy false documents, civilian clothing and for the maintenance of the men during the long journey from Brussels, through Paris to the Spanish frontier as well as railway tickets for the dangerous weary trip. (Darling, D. *Secret Sunday*, William Kimber, (1975), p.35)

In October 1941, when Andrée reappeared in Bilbao with a group of RAF aircrew, she met the MI9 representative who was based in the embassy in Madrid. The valuable aircrew that she brought dispelled any doubts about her. Funding for the line was approved but Andrée insisted that the Comète Line remained under Belgian control. Throughout the war it was organised by Belgian leaders at every stage of the journey from Brussels.

The agreement with the Foreign Office was that Andrée would be reimbursed for her travel costs if she could bring back Allied airmen shot down over Belgium and northern France, escorting them over the Pyrenees. From there, MI9 would arrange their forward trip to the British consulate in Madrid and their entry into Gibraltar or Britain. To assist her, the SIS arranged for Michael Creswell to be sent over to act as her liaison officer. As she used to refer to her charges as 'packages', he nicknamed her 'the Postman'. When she transported an entire seven-man British bomber crew from Belgium to Spain in a week, he renamed her operation "Comet." One of the airmen wrote in his memoirs on the Comète line website that,

> *It was an arduous eight hours trek in silence through the night. The airmen, who were known by members of the line as "the children", often found the journey hard. De Jongh laughs and recalls how sometimes she had to cajole them to carry on. "When one of the men sat down saying he wasn't going any further, I'd try to make him feel ashamed. I understood they hadn't moved for weeks or*

months hiding in houses in Brussels and Paris. It was difficult. But I was a little shocked they weren't trying harder. We couldn't just leave them, either. They would have been found by the Germans and put the whole line in jeopardy. And you know, when you've told someone they can trust you, you say to yourself "I have to get them across. I can't fail." (http://home.clara.net/clinchy/bulletin.htm 22 June 2009)

It was the support of the SIS and the brave efforts of numerous men and women of the Comète line who, over several years and despite many arrests, still devoted time and effort to helping 288 Allied airmen and soldiers get back to Britain. Research by the Comet Kinship association revealed that about 70 pilots were hidden prior to Liberation, about 270 men were in Marathon camps and between 50 and 70 other men were transferred to the 'Val', 'Pat O'Leary' and 'Bourgogne' escape lines. In Neave's *Saturday at MI9,* he commented that

A successful system made it essential that guides escorting the airmen by train should be inconspicuous. Dedée chose young men and women who would pass unnoticed at railway station controls and be able to explain the presence of passengers of Anglo-Saxon appearance who spoke no French. The girls in her organisation were quietly dressed and modest in appearance, but self-possessed. Their looks belied their toughness and resource. The evaders, survivors of air combat, followed them without question…

Dedée became a symbol of courage and defiance during her extraordinary career. Her lively charm and energy won over the most faint-hearted. At the Great Central Hotel, when airmen on their return spoke of her exploits, their eyes filled with tears. I could understand that in these fighting men she inspired not only respect, but also deep affection. They knew that she had saved their lives, and they were afraid for her. So were all those who knew what terrible risks she ran. But Dedée, always determined and independent, kept her own rules. She showed little interest in our admiration. She was possessed by some inner strength. And to the last, she made her own decisions. (**Neave**, op.cit.)

One of Andrée's later passengers, 19-year-old RAF Sergeant Bob Frost, had been shot down in his Wellington Bomber after bombing Essen in autumn 1942. After landing at Kapellen in Brabant, he was sheltered by various families and was back in London within six weeks. In his memoirs on the Comète line website, he remembered the gruelling walk, stumbling around in the dark and wondering how much longer they could go on. Andrée's stamina, he claimed, was clearly extraordinary. Airmen she accompanied often spoke of how much they admired her combination of discretion and energy. Many young men were enormously encouraged by seeing a brave young woman tackle the river crossing and the steep mountain tracks into Spain. Once they were safely on neutral ground, they understood that she was returning to danger.

In Vincent Dujardin and Mark van den Wijngaert's *Léopold III*, they mentioned that there had been a claim made after the war, which they had not been able to substantiate, that, at the end of 1941, Goffinet had ordered Waucquez to leave for Britain to ask the government-in-exile to organise the evacuation of him, the King and all the royal family because they were in danger of being deported to Germany. Research on the Comète line website shows that Goffinet wanted to know whether they should be sent to the Belgian Congo or to England. Waucquez confirmed the claim. The fact that no member of the royal family actually evaded remains a mystery as it gave rise to a major crisis in Belgian politics.

Waucquez agreed to go and on 30 November 1941, he went to check all was safe with Charles Morelle, one of the Comète line workers in Valenciennes and returned to Brussels. A week later Goffinet gave him a personal message written on onion skin paper and a badger shaving brush containing forty pages of microfilm. In appreciation of future British support, Goffinet put his capital in his London bank at the disposal of the Royal Air Force, a continuation of the World War One spirit.

Waucquez landed at Bristol airfield and was taken by car to the Prime Minister Pierlot's house in Woking, Essex, where the precious cargo was revealed to the SIS: three months schedules of rail convoys from Poland to Spain.

A return mission was planned and Waucquez is said to have had SOE training before being flown out of RAF Tempsford on 1 March 1942 on operation BALDRICK. The planned location for the drop was between Orchies and Saint-Amand-les-Eaux at a clearing in Bois de Samain. However, at about 2200 hours, he landed in a farm along the River Scarpe near Marchiennes, a small commune between Douai and Valenciennes, in the Nord département of France. His mission was to set up communication links with various resistance groups and provide financial support for the Comète line. He had funds for the underground press (Libre Belgique, Voice of the Belgians and Vrijschutter) and had to arrange the escape of André De Staercke to take on the role of Chef de Cabinet to Pierlot in London, and Fernand Spaak, the son of Minister of Foreign Affairs.

According to Neave, on 6 May 1942, he and other agents were invited for a meal at Mrs. Roberts' 'safe' house on Street Stévin in Brussels, to celebrate the success of two evaders reaching London. Suddenly the police entered and arrested everyone. However, Adeline Remy, research fellow at the *Laboratoire d'Anthropologie des Mondes Contemporains* told me that the Belgium *Sûreté de l'Etat* files state that Waucquez, Charles Morelle and two agents from London were arrested at Henri Michelli's house on Rue de la Loi in Brussels but that other books suggest it was in his office. Michelli, she told me, was a Belgian who had too many contacts in the resistance.

From the beginning of the war to his involvement in Comet, he had helped with the production and distribution of a clandestine newspaper. Assisted by his son, he had helped 22 officers and soldiers from the Corps Expeditionnaire to escape. He had financially assisted Vladimir Van Damme, the creator of Beaver—an intelligence service group. In late 1941 he became Frederic de Jongh's second-in-command and head of the Brussels section in mid 1942.

These men were, indeed, having dinner together (a very strange habit for clandestine people but not the only one in Comet history. Some members used to regularly have dinner together.).

They had been denounced [to the GFP] *by Flore (Florentine) Giralt (maiden-name)-Dings. She was the mistress of Prosper de Zitter, well-known for having been one of the most productive traitors. They worked for the GFP and the Abwehr. Archives consider these arrests were likely the result of their collaboration.* (Email communication with Adeline Remy, 9 February, 2010)

According to Connart, the arrests undermined the efforts of the *Sicherheitsdienst* (SD) who were making their own enquiries. Waucquez was sentenced to death and imprisoned in Essen, Veckta in Westphalia and Kaisem in Bavaria before being liberated by the Americans in April 1945.

Andrée's father had left Brussels six days earlier. He, like all the men and women involved along the line, risked their lives doing resistance work. The running of the Comète line was taken over by Baron Jean-François Nothomb, known as *Franco.* The Brussels section was taken over by 33-year old Jean Greindl, known as *Nemo* to his friends, who had been working with Andrée since coming back from a coffee plantation in the Congo in 1941. He was helped by Yvon Michiels, known as *Jean* Serment, and Jean Deltour, known as *Jules Dricot.* Their man in Paris was Count Jacques Legrelle, known as *Jérôme.*

With the betrayal of agents in Belgium, Andrée knew

that the Gestapo would soon be looking for her. Accordingly, she dyed her hair black and started being a lot more conscious of being followed.

After the arrests on 6 May, the GFP began shadowing her father in Paris who was working under the assumed name of Monsieur Moreau. Men waiting at railway stations had descriptions of resistance figures who they would look out for at the check points. Suzanne, Andrée's elder sister, was arrested in Brussels on 2 July 1942.

Despite being aware of the consequences, according to the Comète line website, Andrée personally led sixty-four Allied servicemen over the mountains. It was not the most though. Nothomb escorted sixty-seven. However, a single traitor is thought to have been responsible for more than fifty arrests. Frost commented that,

> *"I have nothing but the utmost respect for the people who worked in the Comet Line," he says. "They knew the price if they were caught. It was heroism beyond anything I can tell you. When we got home we could go out, show off our air force wings and lead a normal life. These people could not. They had to remain quiet, carrying on with things and hoping there wasn't going to be a knock on the door."* (Frost, op.cit.)

On the night of 14 January 1943, on her thirty-third trip to Spain, Andrée was betrayed. Information given to the Germans by Prosper Desitter and Jacques Désoubrie, both Belgian renegades, led to her being arrested the next morning with three RAF evaders. (Darling, op.cit. p.194) The farmer, Jean Larburu, was arrested and died in a concentration camp. Frantxa Usandizaga, the owner of a farmhouse in Urrugne, just outside Saint Jean-de-Luz where she used to provide them with bowls of hot milk and soup, was also arrested. The evaders were caught on the last leg of the 1,000 mile (1,600 kms.) journey from Belgium. On her way to a concentration camp in Germany, she was kept in Chateauneuf Prison, the Villa Bayonne, Fort du Hâ in Bordeaux, Fresnes Prison near Paris and Saint-Gilles in Brussels.

There was a stroke of luck as the police were looking for someone with the name 'De Tonga'. Andrée was interrogated eighteen times but never tortured as she had the courage to tell a new set of lies to every set of questions. (Rafferty, op.cit; Darling, D. *Secret Sunday*, Kimber Press, p.101) Eventually, when she admitted that she was the organiser of the Comète escape line, the Gestapo did not believe her. Some suggest that they must have thought she had admitted it to protect a male organiser. Like Franxta, she was transferred to Ravensbrück, the notorious women's concentration camp, where she explained to Wheeler after the war,

> "You go through those huge doors. I can only say it was like entering the gates of hell. It's hard to talk about," she says. "But they didn't break my spirit. I am glad to say I never waxed the SS guards' shoes for an extra bowl of soup, though I was certainly hungry." (http://home.clara.net/clinchy/bulletin.htm 22nd June 2009)

For two years Andrée lived on a diet of dirty potato and turnip soup, practising her nursing skills and trying to avoid being singled out. She was later transferred to Mauthausen but Franxta died there. Gravely ill and undernourished, she was released by the advancing Allied armies in April 1945 but many of her colleagues died in captivity.

Andrée's father carried on in the line after her arrest, moving the headquarters to his school in the Place Gaucheret, now called École Frédéric de Jongh, until February 1942. In that month the Luftwaffe's Secret Police, incensed by reports of airmen escaping and returning to fly again, increased their vigilance. German Commanders-in-Chief in Belgium and France published orders making it a capital offence to hide or assist Allied prisoners-of-war. From then on the Gestapo and Abwehr launched a determined attempt to infiltrate and destroy the escape lines. Neave commented in *Saturday at MI9* that,

> "*It was to be a grim combat which cost many lives. The intervention of the Luftwaffe was significant. It is known that Goering* (the head of the Luftwaffe) *realised the existence of secret escape organisations for recovering of R.A.F. pilots and crews. He must have known its value to the Allied Air Forces. He gave orders that it was to be crushed.*" (Neave, op.cit.)

Eventually Frédéric was betrayed, arrested at Gare du Nord, a Paris railway station on 6/7 June 1943. He was shot at Mont Valérian in Paris on 28 March 1944, a spot which President Charles de Gaulle inaugurated in 1960 as a French Memorial for Resistance fighters and deported people.

Many hundreds of helpers were similarly arrested. A few hundred are thought to have died in concentration camps. Many others were executed in Germany, including Andrée's boss, Baron Jacques Donny.

Neave recalled sitting in a first-class compartment on the train south from Paris with '*this quite remarkable girl*' (whose) '*… movements were quick and definite as were her thoughts and repartee … 'She seemed to be always smiling and brimful of enthusiasm.*' He considered her to have been '*one of our greatest agents*'. Another appreciative evader wrote of her as being '*the force, the power and the inspiration that brought us from Belgium to Spain.*'

After the war, she was one of four Belgian women awarded the George Medal by the British. She was one of many given the Medal of Freedom by the Americans, and the Croix de Guerre with palm by the Belgians. She was also created Chevalier of the French Legion d'Honneur and awarded the Belgian Order of Léopold. All Belgian agents were soldiers in the "*Compagnie des Subsistant*", a cover administrative unit, and given a rank. After the war she was considered an ARA, "Agent de Renseignement et Action" and was the only woman among the four Belgian lieutenant-colonels ever commissioned during World War Two.

Jean Greindl refused to leave when advised by Neave, insisting that the Comète line's principal guides got out first. One of whom, red-headed Peggy van Lier, had been arrested and interrogated by "*a fat, evil, rat-faced SS officer*". In her obituary in *The Telegraph,* it stated that his questions were countered with the same cool which had seen her through numerous dangerous situations. When she was told that she could go, she was so astonished that she shook her interrogator's hand. Horrified at what she had done, she burst into tears as soon as she left his office.

Desperate to continue her work, Greindl had refused, arguing that the Gestapo knew her. He insisted that Peggy followed the same route that she had helped evaders to get out of France. One report has it that she was smuggled into Gibraltar in the bilges of a boat full of oranges.

> *As she stepped down from an RAF transport at Hendon airfield, Peggy van Lier was greeted on behalf of MI9 by Jimmy Langley, a handsome young Guards officer who in 1940 had lost an arm at Dunkirk and been taken prisoner.*
>
> *He had then escaped from a German military hospital at Lille, made his way across France under his own initiative, and after reaching Marseilles operated with an escape line before being repatriated in 1941. He soon became an important figure at MI9, where he worked closely with Airey Neave.*
>
> *On this particular Sunday in January 1943, Langley was not best pleased to be dispatched to Hendon in place of Neave, who was then on his honeymoon. But Langley was instantly captivated by the fresh face and blue eyes of Peggy van Lier. The pair fell in love, and within a year Neave was standing in for Langley while he was on his honeymoon.*
>
> *Meanwhile, Neave and Langley had learned how Peggy van Lier had operated under the cover*

of a Swedish Red Cross canteen run by Greindl which provided food and clothes for poor children in Brussels. Her position there had allowed her to team up with Andrée de Jongh, Comet's intrepid founder. (http://www.telegraph.co.uk/news/obituaries/1349750/Peggy-Langley.html   2nd   July 2009)

After the war, Peggy Langley was appointed MBE and awarded the Belgian Croix de Guerre with Palm. She also held other Belgian decorations and the Netherlands Resistance Cross.

Greindl was arrested on 6 February 1943 at the Swedish canteen and executed on 7 September that year. On the day following Deltour's arrest on 16 January 1944, the Gestapo picked up Nothomb and Legrelle. Nothomb survived several concentration camps and was awarded the Distinguished Service Order.

According to the comete-bidossoa website, another woman who worked on the Comète line and got out was Yvonne Lapeyre. She and her husband had both helped Tante Go by letting evaders stay at their house and escorting them to the next. They were very lucky as, at five o'clock in the morning on 11 March 1943, a Gestapo team found the right building in Bayonne but broke into the wrong apartment. It was agreed that they should leave the country and work for the line in London until the heat had died down. They did and returned in 1945.

As we have seen, the Comète line operated on a system using mainly young girls as couriers who took evaders between safe houses by train, bicycle and on foot. Many of these couriers were caught and suffered badly under the Gestapo and the concentration camp system. Many never returned. One of Andrée's early couriers was Andrée Dumon, known as Nadine, who made many journeys from Brussels to Paris. On one occasion she took twenty Americans. According to Ameline Remy, her father worked mainly for the Luc-Marc Intelligence Service group which collaborated with Frederic de Jong in transferring aircrews to the escape line.

In August 1942, Andrée Dumon was arrested with her parents at her home and interrogated. The Germans had infiltrated the line and she had been betrayed. They knew exactly who she was and what her family was doing. After twelve months in prisons and small camps in Essen, Zweibrücken, Mesum and Gross-Sterlitz she was transferred to Ravensbrück in January 1945 and Mauthausen in February where she was eventually liberated in April.

Recognising the need of continuing the line, Andrée's older sister, 19-year-old Ailine, took over the role. Better known as Michou, she became one of the line's most successful operators between 1943 and 1944. In memory of some of those rescued by the Dumons, the 91stbombgroup website commented about Michou that following,

> the great wave of arrests in 1943 she became a sort of odd-job woman: looking for hide-outs, escorting pilots, recruiting new agents, collecting food coupons, to restore the escape route after each wave of arrests. She had a thorough knowledge of the whole line. If due to other circumstances there was a shortage of agents she joined in. Five times she crossed the Pyrenees with fugitives. Time and again she succeeded to escape the Gestapo, thanks to her cold-bloodedness, insight, and to a certain extent a certain dose of good luck. (http://www.91stbombgroup.com/91st_info/schweinfurt_raid. html, 2 July 2009)

Neave was impressed by Michou saying that, "*Amongst her many gallant services she brought ten men over the frontier between December 1943 and May 1944.*" Eventually, when the Gestapo were closing in, Michou escaped down her own line, reaching London in May 1944. After the war, the Allies showed their gratitude towards all those involved in helping crashed aircrews escape back to England. Andrée de Jong, Marie Louise Dissard, Frédérique Dupuich and Micheline Dumon were awarded the George Medal, the highest civilian decoration during World War Two. Andrée Dumon was awarded the OBE. Micheline and Elvire de Greef were each awarded the US Medal of Freedom with Gold Palm.

The Comète line website mentions 288 'aviators' and seventy-three civilians were successfully got out whereas in the Escape Room at the Lincolnshire Aviation Heritage Centre it claims it returned 773 people, mostly Allied soldiers and airmen but also 216 agents. Dedèe personally took 118 to safety in 25 crossings. There was no mention of any women. The last evaders down this line were two RAF sergeants who reached Spain in early June 1944. A few months later, after the Allied invasion of Normandy on D-Day, three women parachuted into Belgium and northern France on top secret missions.

It is worth mentioning that in Neave's *Saturday at M.I.9,* he tells how the Comète line worked alongside the PAT escape line. It had been established by Ian Garrow, a soldier in the British Army, who had missed the Dunkirk evacuation and remained in France. When he was arrested in October 1941, the network was taken over by Albert Guérisse, a Belgian military doctor, known by the alias Pat O'Leary. He had escaped to England, was trained by the SOE and sent back to help organise another escape line. Although initially based near Perpignan, his network had safe houses in Paris, Marseilles and Toulouse. The PAT line got evaders out from southeast France, either by boat from the Mediterranean coast, or over the eastern Pyrenees into Spain. When O'Leary was arrested in March 1943, Mary Louise Dissard, like Andrée de Jongh, took over the reins and continued the western side of the operation. She was a 62-year-old member of the resistance from Toulouse who the Germans never suspected as being involved until one of the evaders was captured along with a notebook containing her name and address. Forced to go into hiding, she lived in attics, cellars and garages until Toulouse was liberated on 15 August 1944.

SOE and the Belgian Country Section

In the summer of 1940, after the evacuation from Dunkirk, the Secret Intelligence Service (SIS) of the British Foreign Office, approached the Air Ministry with the suggestion that they experiment in how feasible it would be to parachute agents and land aircraft to pick up VIPs (Very Important Persons) from occupied countries who could be useful for the war effort. As has been mentioned, many persons of great value to Britain and her allies had been left behind when the Germans overran France and the Low Countries. Some key trained individuals were said to have been deliberately left behind and planted among the local communities. They merged into the local population and helped train them clandestinely to oppose the German assimilation of the conquered territories. It was essential that some of these people occasionally needed to be brought back to England for additional training and then sent back to help the resistance groups.

Winston Churchill, Britain's Prime Minister at the time, recognised the urgency of the situation and agreed. The Special Operations Executive (SOE) was created with a directive "to set Europe ablaze." Those 'in the know' called it the Inter-Services Research Bureau. Two RAF 'Special Duties Squadrons were formed. Initially, they were based on Newmarket racecourse and used short take-off and landing, single-engined Westland Lysanders and twin-engined Armstrong Whitworth Whitley bombers. When RAF Tempsford became available in October 1941, other planes were brought into use including the much larger Short Stirling and the Handley Page Halifax bomber. However, they had to be specially converted to carry, not bombs, but supplies for the resistance as well as parachutists who would be dropped in the early hours of the morning on moonlit nights.

Pilots had to learn how to fly low and without lights. A top secret airfield was built near Tempsford, a small agricultural village in a remote area between Cambridge and Bedford, about fifty miles (80 kms.) north of London. Said to have been designed by Jasper Maskelyne, an illusionist, to resemble a disused airfield, eventually over two thousand personnel were based there.

Some of the farm labourers cottages and farm buildings were demolished. The roof slates of Gibraltar Farm were removed to make it look derelict. Windows had the glass deliberately broken. Sacks were draped across the inside of the windows instead of curtains. The doors were left rickety. For the same reason much of the black Bedfordshire weather-boarding was removed. The adjacent farm buildings got the same treatment and visitors reported them being mildewed, cobwebbed and covered in mouldering thatch.

Some suggest tarpaulins were draped over hangars and new buildings on which agricultural buildings had been painted to blend in with the surrounding farmland. Some were said to have been thatched. Inside Gibraltar Farm it was said that the stairs, ceiling and first floor were removed to create a very large room. The inside walls were built up and reinforced to withstand bomb damage. This was to be the airfield's nerve centre. Nissen huts resembled pig sties and cow sheds. Outside Gibraltar Farm, the pond was left with the odd few ducks. Genuine tractors were left but moved occasionally in the fields and yards. The runways were painted with green or brown patches to look like they were overgrown. In some places a thick black line was painted across the runway, to give overflying pilots the impression that it was the continuation of the hedge. Cattle were deliberately grazed on some of the fields when the runways were not in use to make the pilots of any German planes that managed to fly over think it was used for agricultural purposes. To make it more difficult to be spotted, planes only ever took off on the nights on either side of the full moon. The plan succeeded. It is said that the aerial photographs taken by German pilots who flew over were interpreted as a disused airfield. Not one bomb was dropped on it, only a flare on the runway one night.

The Lysanders needed modifying to carry secret agents to fields within a five hundred mile (800 kms.) or so distance from the English coast. An additional fuel tank containing 150 gallons was attached between the wheel arches. A ladder was welded onto the left hand side of the fuselage to facilitate passengers easier access with their luggage. Outbound passengers were the secret agents; inbound included military personnel, politicians, industrialists, downed pilots and aircrew, secret agents who had been in 'The Field' and needed bringing back as well as resistance members who needed training or safety if they were being hunted by the Gestapo. It was not uncommon for women agents to be sent out and, if they evaded capture, brought back. Sometimes women, like wives and girlfriends of influential politicians, industrialists and resistance figures, were exfiltrated. Details can be found in my books, *'The Women of RAF Tempsford'* and *'Churchill's Angels'*.

As Lysanders could only carry two passenger, three at a crush, King George allocated his royal plane, a twin-engined Lockheed Hudson and his pilot, Edward 'Mouse' Fielden, to the Special Duties Squadrons at Tempsford. This plane could carry up to a dozen passengers, much more comfortably and for a much further distance than the Lysanders.

Once the runways at Tempsford were ready in October 1941, the Special Duties Squadrons were based there. 138 Squadron dropped supplies and parachutists whilst 161 Squadron, which did the Lysander pick-ups, flew down to RAF Tangmere, near Chichester on the south coast of England and were based there during the moon period.

When President Roosevelt brought the Americans into the war in 1943, he allocated the 492nd Bomb Group of the 8th Air Force the task of helping SOE in its work. They became known as the 'Carpetbaggers'. Their pilots and crews, who had little, if any, experience of flying low and by night, needed training. Consequently, they spent a month at what they called 'The Tempsford Academy', accompanying RAF crews on two missions before transferring to their own air base at RAF Harrington, near Kettering in Northamptonshire.

The Office of Strategic Services (OSS), the American equivalent of the SIS, which was to become the CIA after the Second World War, organised their own 'Joes'. These were the men and women who were to be sent into the field. They also took over the Packing Group, ensuring that all the containers destined for the resistance groups had the right contents. Under the command of the Supreme Headquarters Allied Expeditionary Force (SHAEF), they flew over 3,000 sorties to drop over 7,000 tons of supplies to 350,000 resistance members in occupied Europe.

Other functions of SOE included 'unattributable' industrial sabotage, the raising and supplying of secret armies and collecting intelligence information, all done under what Michael Foot, the SOE historian, describes as *'the dense fog of secrecy'*. Its five floor office block, situated at 64 Baker Street in London W.1., had to have War Department cover so the name 'MOI (SP)' was coined and its telephone number added to the War Office's directory. Captain Peter Lee, an officer in its security section said *"it was terribly clever. We said it stood for 'Mysterious Operations In Special Places'. We reckoned the Germans, with their lack of sense of humour, would never be able to unravel that one."*

Like the Belgian government-in-exile relocated to London, so too did other governments. Consequently, the SOE set up different country sections near its HQ. Belgium was T Section, Holland was N, France was F and de Gaulle's Free French was RF. In Major Graham T. R. Thompson's memoirs about the Belgian Country Section, he said that its executive was based in three rooms at Norgeby House, 83 Baker Street. A fourth room was used by the three civilian women secretaries, which he thought was an inconvenient arrangement.

The Head of Section (T.) was Mr. Dadson who, apart from general supervision, looked after matters of policy, top relations with the Belgian Services, and, of course, plans in general for our operations. He was responsible to the Director for Western Europe. A Mr. Duff-Torrance was in charge of operations, briefing, preparation of missions, and communications with agents in the field, with the help of a secretary. The remaining sub-section, in the charge of Major Claude Knight, dealt with pretty nearly everything not covered by Messrs. Dadson and Duff-Torrance. This included recruiting, training (by liaison with the Training (M.) Section), general disposal of agents between and after school courses, a good deal of liaison with the Belgian Services at most levels, cover, clothing, and arrangements (in liaison with the Military Operations (MO.) Section) for despatch, and many other miscellaneous duties. For this work Major Knight had, in addition to a Secretary, a Captain Jocelyn Clarke, a number of Conducting Officers at the various Special Training Schools, and myself.

Clarke's work and mine were roughly interchangeable at this time and, apart from the general rush of work in London, which I described briefly in my earlier notes, we visited various schools periodically for short stays to see how our men were getting on with their training. In addition, we took it in turns to accompany departing agents to the climbed into the plane. The term used in our Section for this latter work was Accompanying Officer. The men in training were usually sent to the schools in batches for a course of definite duration, and it was customary for each batch to be accompanied by a Conducting Officer and a Field Security N.C.O. [Non Commissioned Officer] (www.thompsononename.org.uk/pdf/SOE.pdf 27th June 2009)

The Dutch, French and other country sections were in

the same building and the signals and cipher staff were in Michael House, about 200 metres away. The men Thompson were referring to were those identified as potential secret agents. Whilst those that avoided capture played a vital role in the eventual liberation of Belgium, I am going to be focusing more on the women who went through the same training schools. Whilst some of the other agents sent into Belgium may have been resident in the UK before the war, I suspect that many would have been drawn from the Belgian armed forces who had managed to get across the Channel from Dunkirk and camped in Tenby, North Wales. Some had business or commercial interests in Belgium and its colonies before the war, whilst others might have been got out along the Comète line. All had to be fluent in French. Flemish would have been a bonus, as would an understanding of German.

After being interviewed to identify their willingness to join the 'Inter Services Research Bureau' they had to sign the 'Poison Book', the term used for the Official Secrets Act. Any information that they might subsequently divulge about their work would be punishable by imprisonment. Training was described by Thompson as like starting in Lower Third and ending in the Sixth Form except compressed into several months. Their assessment course was held at Winterfold, a secluded country house at the foot of the Surrey Hills between Guildford and Horsham.

Here, apart from being observed to assess their social skills and leadership qualities, they underwent thorough physical training, were taught the rudiments of fieldcraft (outdoor survival), given weapons training and rudimentary exercises in using explosives. Whilst undergoing training they were given a cover name, so that their real name was not known to fellow students. The theory was that this avoided repercussions for their families should agents be captured in the field and succumb to torture. In practice, agents sometimes knew each other from before the war.

Students could eat and drink as much as they liked but, their 'accompanying'. 'escorting' or 'conducting officer' made careful note on how they behaved, even their table manners. They were encouraged to drink, but if they got drunk and talked too much about their real life or were too critical of the system, they would fail. Unsuitable candidates went back to normal work, none the wiser about the real work of SOE. A few days leave in London or back home was probably very welcome.

Elaine, Olga and Frédérique in all likelihood, would have understood Nancy Wake's description of Winterfold as 'The Mad House'. The types of exercises they were given made many 'students' wonder at the reasons behind them. Obstacle courses were laid out with various objects like tyres, nets, logs and barrels were set out and labelled A, B and C. One student might be told to climb over all the As, go clockwise round the Bs and anticlockwise round the Cs whilst a second student had to go clockwise round the As, go anti-clockwise round the Bs and climb over the Cs. Other tasks included using whatever means they could to cross a large pond without getting their feet wet, traversing a large wooden frame without letting their feet touching the ground and group work carrying full water butts across a lawn without spilling any. There were memory games where they were shown a tray with dozens of objects which they had to memorise. The tray was then taken away and one item removed and, when it was brought back, students had to identify which item was missing. They might be given a photograph to study and then be asked to describe in detail what was in it. Someone was brought into the class; they had to study them and, when they had gone, a detailed description of them had to be given.

What puzzled many were the psychological tests. They were taken into an office, sat down and shown an assortment of ink blots on cards which, spontaneously, they had to suggest what shapes they resembled. Their responses were written down. Presumably, their answers shed light on their personality. Elaine commented that she thought it was a 'loony bin', a lunatic asylum. Once the 'assessment' was finished they were returned home to await a decision.

Those assessed as being suitable material were notified by post or telephone and sent a rail pass with a note to rendezvous at Euston Station in London. There they would meet their conducting officer and board the night train to Edinburgh from where they changed for Fort William and Arisaig, a remote estate in Inverness-shire on the northwest coast of Scotland. Here they were accommodated in one of eleven shooting lodges for three or four weeks paramilitary training, what was called 'the art of ungentlemanly warfare', The courses included yet more physical training, silent killing, weapons handling, grenade throwing, knife work, rope work, boat work, demolition of railway engines, railway lines and bridges, map reading, compass work, field craft (outdoor survival), more Morse code, burglary, key cutting, forgery, learning how to jump off moving trains and advanced raid tactics.

Like at Winterfold, there was no rationing, the diet being augmented by freshly caught fish, crab, mackerel, mussels and oysters. Occasionally a hand grenade tossed into a river might have killed a salmon or a good shot with a rifle brought down a deer. The local hotel and pubs were not off-limits and bottles of whisky were not in short supply.

Their instructors and conducting officer wrote reports on their skill and aptitude, recommending whether they were suitable for clandestine work. Those who failed this course were sent to 'The Cooler', either a remote country estate at Inverlair, where they made mountaineering equipment for the duration of the war, or one near Guildford. What they had learned had not to be revealed to the general public until it was deemed safe for them to be 'released'. And then, having signed the Official Secrets Act, they would be expected to 'keep mum', tell no-one.

After a farewell party to which many girls from outlying villages and fishing ports were brought in, the agents caught the train to Manchester. Often buses were hired to take them to their next course, parachute training at Ringway airfield (STS 51), about twelve miles (25 km) south of Manchester.

After completing her preliminary training, Elaine was

called back to T Section. It was only then that she learned just what was expected of her. In her interview for the TV documentary, *The Children who Fought Hitler,* she recalled the SOE officer saying:

> *'Ok. You have done well in all your courses. Now we go to Ringway.' 'Ringway? 'Yes, for the parachute jumping.' 'Parachute jumping.' I must have gone white in the face. And he looked at me and he said 'Yes, of course. ... How do you think we get you to Belgium? And I thought, Belgium? Now? And he said, 'What do you think... what are you're doing here?' I didn't know. I had no idea I was going to go to Belgium. He got into such a filthy rage. 'How the hell did you get in here? Now that you've passed all your training. We can't kick you out. What are we going to do with you? Are you too bloody scared to jump from an aeroplane? And he got me so annoyed. I was stamping my feet. 'I will jump. I will jump.' And he said, 'God. If you don't jump there'll be hell waiting for you.' So off I went to Ringway.* (Elliot, S. and Fox, J. (2009), *The Children who Fought Hitler,* John Murray)

During the time they spent there, up a week depending on the weather, they were accommodated either at Dunham House (STS 51a), near Altrincham, Fulshaw Hall (STS 51b), near Wilmslow, or York House (STS 51c), near Timperley. To get their 'wings', as well as more physical training, they had to master jumping and landing from increasing heights and complete at least three drops from an air balloon and two from an airplane into the grounds of the adjoining estate of Tatton Park. At least one drop was at night. Once the course was completed they were given a few days leave in London.

The commandoes in the Belgian Independent Parachute Company were stationed at Malvern, Worcestershire where they were trained for their missions by the Special Air Service (SAS). Their parachute training was at Ringway. Having won their wings, agents were given some opportunities for rest and recreation. According to Thompson,

> *At intervals during their training, agents were provided with breaks in London, when they would be lodged individually in one of a large number of security-covered hotels - the type of hotel being arranged to suit the background of the man. The object of these breaks was two-fold, firstly to maintain morale by letting the man enjoy some recreation in the then not so bright lights of London.* (Thompson, op.cit.)

As we shall see, Frédérique did not attend Ringway but all the agents would have been driven down the A3 for three or four weeks' intensive 'spy training' at what was called the 'Finishing School'. It was at Beaulieu (pronounced Bewley) Abbey, an 8,000 estate in the New Forest, close to Bournemouth on the South Coast. Here they were accommodated in one of seven requisitioned large country houses hidden away in the park. No wonder many agents described the SOE as standing for 'Stately 'Omes of England'. As well as more physical training, students were taught the art of fieldcraft, use of British and enemy weapons as well as specialist classes in 'spycraft', identifying enemy uniforms, avoiding detection, breaking and entering, blowing safes open, forgery and disguises. They were even given experience of withstanding Gestapo interrogation.

The methods used were rather realistic reconstructions. Elaine commented that hers was humiliating. After having been woken up in the early hours of the morning by one of her trainers dressed in German uniform, she was told she was a prisoner and had to go accompany him downstairs to the interrogation room. Some women referred to being taken to the kitchen. Elaine described it as a big, dark room with a big headlight shining down on a table, behind which sat three German officers.

> *I was in pyjamas having been just taken straight out of my bed. ...Then they started interrogating me. They made me stand up on a chair and I was standing on this chair with a big floodlight into my eyes. And they made me take off my pyjama jacket and went on interrogating so I just had my pyjama trousers on and I was bare from the waist up on this damn chair thinking what the hell are they playing at. ...and then they turned the lights on and all the other students were sitting around .When the lights went on they all started clapping because there I was, bare-breasted, standing on this chair. I could have killed them.* (Elliot, S. and Fox, J. op.cit.)

Some days they were sent into Southampton or Bournemouth with a mission to undertake. It might be to rendezvous with someone, pass on a message, find out information, catch a particular train, jump out at a particular point and report back to the house before a particular time, all the while ensuring that they were not followed. They had to learn from their mistakes.

The Belgian men would have been approached by particularly attractive women, specially chosen to test the agents' suitability for clandestine work. This was called the 'honey pot' trap. After a good meal and plenty of alcohol, they might be invited to bed and subtly questioned as to what exercises they had been doing, who the other students were and what their teachers were like. If their pillow talk let slip 'sensitive' information, they would fail the course. There is no evidence suggesting that any women agents had attractive men try and seduce information out of them.

The majority of the women agents trained as couriers. It was said that the upper echelons of the Dutch section of the SOE, as late as 1944, thought that women were rarely stopped or searched at controls and that they were rarely picked up in mass arrests. That was the case in France early in the war but, as it progressed, most women were stopped and searched as well. What was true was that they made excellent cover whilst travelling around the country taking messages, papers, money, wireless equipment or explosives, pretending to be going shopping, foraging for food or visiting friends. It was thought that the Germans wouldn't expect women to be involved in Resistance activities. They were expected to be fulfilling the traditional roles of 'Kinder, Kirche und Küche (Children, Church and Kitchen). They were slow to realise that young, attractive women could be politicised and intent on carrying out deadly work.

Whilst there were circumstances when a bike was vital for getting around, for long journeys it was recommended that the women travelled first class on the trains, as the Germans were less likely to thoroughly search wealthy middle class passengers than those in third class compartments. Big businessmen and Germans who travelled in first class didn't want the police to annoy them. The women were taught to hide incriminating items where they would least likely to be found. False bottomed bags, inside bicycle frames or bicycle tyres, under dress belts, under the soles of stockings, inside powder compacts or even inside long hair had less chance of detection during perfunctory searches. Hiding objects internally was another possibility. However, should their cover story be doubted, they had to expect a full body search.

Women were also thought to be more resourceful and composed than men and could talk themselves better out of tight spots at check points using their feminine charms. They were also more inventive, conjuring ingenious cover stories. Questions they had to be able to answer were 'Where did you get your laundry cleaned?' or ' Where did you get your hair done?'

Those women who were married may well have used an imaginary husband in their cover story. Unmarried women would probably have been provided with imaginary boyfriends. Major Thompson, in his memoirs '*The SOE in Belgium*' admitted being an 'accompanying' or 'conducting officer'. With the assistance of a competent secretary, Miss Lee-Graham, later Mrs Koslowska but known only to the agents as 'Mrs Cameron,' they devised ingenious cover stories.

> We considered that most men would look more normal with a little love life and interest, so letters and photographs of girls were provided for men who wished it. The photographs initially provided some difficulty, but one which was solved for us involuntarily by one of our trainees. Unknown to us at the time, a man on leave in London from one of our schools contrived to insert an advertisement in a Quebec newspaper: "Lonely Belgium soldier wishes to find girl pen friend." The resulting replies were intercepted by our Security and of course the man could not be allowed to have them. We were, consequently, put in possession of a vast assortment of letters, most of which enclosed photographs of attractive young French Canadian girls, often signed on the back (and we had others signed ourselves!) Of these, many were suitable to provide fictitious girl friends for our men, and they could choose from a selection the girl that they preferred. I do not suppose that many French Canadian girls will ever know how usefully they unwittingly contributed to the allied war effort in their youth! (www.thompsononename.org.uk/pdf/SOE.pdf 27 June 2009)

Some women reported that they were not allowed spirits whilst at Beaulieu but drinking local beer was much more common. One group, when last orders was called, was said to have had forty pints lined up along the counter in the bar and not being allowed to go to sleep until they had all been drunk. Woe betide anyone who was awoken in the night and was not talking Flemish or French. All the lessons were in Flemish or French; the reading material was in Flemish or French and they even listened to Radio Belgium.

Before they finished the course, they were given a two or three day 'schedule' where they had to visit a town or city, sometimes a long distance away, identify suitable 'safe' houses, choose dead letter boxes, maybe break into a building, steal or photograph documents and rendezvous with contacts, all the time ensuring that they were never followed.

There was also training in getting on and off Lysander and Hudson airplanes for those who were not going to be parachuted in. Those whose job might include training reception committees in parachute drops or landings needed to learn how to arrange the lights for the flarepath.

Depending on the type of specialist training the SOE, SIS or the OSS deemed necessary for their agents to have, they were sent to one of a number of specialist training schools.

Agents sent to Gumley Hall (STS 44), an eighteenth century mansion near Market Harborough in Leicestershire, with forty-five bedrooms set in 2,000 acres, received intensive weapons training and further unarmed combat lessons under the command of Major J. H. Drumbell. Those destined for industrial sabotage work went to the seventeenth century Brickendonbury Manor (STS 17), near Hertford in Hertfordshire. Initially under the command of Captain Frederic Peters and then by Colonel George Rheam, students were taught exactly which part of a factory, power station, telephone exchange, railway, dock or shipyard to target, exactly where to place the explosives, what quantities to use and which type of time pencil - the half hour, one hour, two hour or longer.

Those identified as potential wireless or radio operators were sent to Thame Park (STS 52), in Oxfordshire for intensive wireless and security training using the most up-to-date equipment. The SOE 'boffins' were constantly improving radio communications technology. Agents had to be able to type messages in Morse Code at between eighteen and twenty-two words per minute, to encode and decipher messages accurately and use appropriate safety checks in their transmissions to let headquarters know they were still safe. Missing them out would indicate they were operating under duress or that someone else was typing. As we shall see, this was a very serious problem for the T Section's agents.

Some might have been sent to Howbury Hall (STS 40), near Bedford, where they would have been given specialist training in using Eureka, Rebecca and S-Phones, the latest ground-to-air communication equipment.

During their briefing sessions for their missions, agents stayed in houses or flats rented by T section in and around London. Thompson recorded booking rooms initially at Fitzmaurice Place but, as the war progressed, another was found at 25 Edgware Road because rooms were being used for briefing and debriefing Belgian 'representatives'. Some would have been successfully returned Comète line evaders who had up-to-the-minute information about life under occupation.

Their conducting officer arranged visits to hairdressers to ensure the style was correct for Belgium, took them to the dentist to replace any fillings with Belgian-looking ones, took them to the SOE clothes warehouse to ensure that every single item of clothing they were taking was appropriate for Belgium. They even ensured that, if they smoked they had Belgian tobacco and had Belgium soap and fragrances. Prior to their flight out from Tempsford, agents were encouraged to write their will, just in case! They were encouraged to write letters and postcards that would be posted to their family and friends at regular intervals whilst they were in the field. They had to be prepared to live a new identity, provided with cover, ration cards and essential papers. Thompson pointed out that

> "... gradually, the Cover Story was to become a much more organised and scientific affair. Discussions with the agent would be started as soon as he left the preliminary Training School, and a long and pains-taking build-up would continue right through his training, until the results met with his and my satisfaction, and finally with the satisfaction

of an examining interrogator immediately before his departure. (Ibid.)

They were kept up-to-date with news from Belgium, the latest films, radio programmes, curfew times, ration cards and other permits needed so as not to give anyone the impression that they had just arrived from England. They had to fit seamlessly back into normal society. Their 'conducting officer' would also go over their cover story, the role they had to adopt back in Belgium, and carefully examine photographs and maps of the 'drop zone'.

Once fully briefed as to their mission, agents were kept until the flight was ready at what were called 'Holding Stations' or 'Holding Schools'. Here they were provided with high class 'Rest and Recreation'. There were no holds barred except, as far as I can determine, sex and drugs. The Belgian agents were accommodated with the Dutch at the 18th Chicheley Hall (STS 20) near Newport Pagnell in Buckinghamshire, described as one of England's finest and loveliest English country houses.

Within a week of Thompson joining the Belgian Section in September 1941, he,

> *...was taken down to our Holding School at Chicheley where I met a very tough, commando-type bunch of trained saboteurs under the command of Colonel Roper-Caldbeck and looked after by Lieut. Ivor Dobson, one of our Section Conducting Officers. These men, mostly Flemish-speaking, were all fully trained and anxious to go into the field, but it was not the policy, at that stage in the war, to embark on extensive sabotage in occupied Europe, so the men had to be kept in a Holding School, given some routine training, and generally kept occupied and amused.* (Ibid.)

In late-1941, the location of the 'Holding School' was changed. Another large house was available which became known as the 'Despatching School'. It was in the mansion at Audley End (STS 43), near Saffron Walden, about twenty-five miles (40 kms.) from Newmarket. The agents were usually taken there on the day of departure or the preceding afternoon. Normally, their stay there was very short unless the weather forecast meant their flight was cancelled or sometimes, if the pilot was unable to pinpoint the drop zone or the reception committee on the ground flashed the wrong identification letter or was missing, the agents were returned to base.

> *In spite of the seriousness of the business in hand, the atmosphere of Audley End was informal and delightful. The domestic arrangements were in the hands of a Mrs. Gregson with her attractive staff of young F.A.N.Y.s, doing cooking, housework and driving. The men were mostly housed in dormitories, keeping as far as possible to their own nationalities.* (Ibid.)

Other nationalities were taken to West Court (STS 6), a fine 17th century mansion at Finchampstead Lea, near Reading in Berkshire. What might now be called 'Rest and Recreation' was provided by attractive young women in the FANY. Fine food and wine, dancing, chatting, playing games of ping pong, dominoes or cards and listening to the wireless might while away the hours whilst they waited. Two eggs on their plate was the unwritten message that their mission was on that night. A blacked-out car would arrive after dinner and the FANY would drive the agents and their conducting officers to the airfield which would be ready to take them to Belgium.

Later in the war, Belgian agents were housed in Gaynes Hall (STS 61), near St. Neots. A FANY (First Aid Nursing Yeomanry) driver would take them the less than an hour's drive in her curtain-drawn car to Gibraltar Farm on Tempsford Airfield. Their conducting officer might take them inside where they would have a last chance to examine the photographs of their drop zone. Then they would be taken across the farmyard to the barn. Any loose change was 'contributed' to the RAF Benevolent Fund. Pockets would be emptied and soles of their shoes checked for anything that might link them to England if they were caught. They were then kitted up with a padded 'striptease' jump suit over which a parachute and harness was attached. A padded helmet, gloves and boots were provided. Money for the resistance groups, sometimes millions in forged currency, was stuffed into their pockets or a money belt. Sometimes a spade was attached to their leg, which would be used to bury the parachute after they landed. They then were given the choice of a revolver or double-sided knife and a selection of pills.

Terry Crowdy in his *SOE AGENT: Churchill's Secret Warriors*, listed them. 'A' pills were for airsickness. 'B' pills containing Benzedrine were for use as a stimulant. The amphetamine Mecrodrin was also issued. Both could be used to keep people awake, especially radio operators who had early morning transmissions and reception committees. The 'E' pills: were a quick-working anaesthetic that would knock a person out for 30 seconds; 'K' pills were used for inducing longer periods of sleep. 'L' pills, should they accept them, were lethal potassium cyanide crystals in a biteable-through thin rubber coating and hidden in the top inside part of their jacket, in hollowed out wine bottle corks or tubes of lipstick. You would be dead in fifteen seconds if chewed, longer if swallowed. Agents were told that the Catholic Church had given them a special dispensation to use the pill 'in extremis'.

The final thing they were given was a good luck gift. This might be gold cuff-links, cigarette case, powder compact or a piece of jewellery – a reminder that SOE was thinking of them. When they ran out of money they were told it could be pawned or sold on the black market. Some of these smaller items were used to conceal codes, messages and microscopic photographs. Hiding places included fountain pens, pencils, wallets, bath salts, shaving sticks, toothpaste tubes, talcum powder boxes, lipsticks, manicure sets, sponges, penknives, shoe heels and soles, shoulder padding, collar studs, coat buttons, and cigarette lighters.

In Michael Foot's *SOE in the Low Countries*, he stated that T Section had sent forty-five agents into Belgium by late October 1942. Only one, Henri Verhaegen had got back to England and only three missions were said to have been successful. *"Thirty-two had fallen into enemy hands, ten of them—including three killed in action– on their dropping zones. Besides Leblicq, who had never landed, eighteen of these forty-five were wireless operators."* (Foot, M. *SOE in the Low Countries*, St Ermins Press, (2001), p. 295) How many of the twenty-five wireless transmitters in operation at the end of 1942 were in Germans hands and being played back to London, as they were in Holland, is unknown.

The SOE believed that loss of radio operators was due to successful direction finding techniques by German radio goniometrists. Operators were transmitting for too long. Fifteen minutes was considered long enough. However, the vast majority of arrests in Belgium were said to have been from 'delation', people informing the Germans about radio operators and agents in the hope of a large financial reward. Millions were offered for information leading to the arrest of resistance leaders, less for radio operators and couriers but, for some Belgians, it was a tempting offer.

Extracting information from captured agents and careless talk doubtless led to other arrests. Another factor was the German's using Fieseler Storch aircraft, which, like the Lysander, could fly low and identify potential drop zones and listen in on the reception committee's S-phone, its ground-to-air radio communication.

By the end of the war, 182 agents had been sent into Belgium, of whom sixty-one - one in three - were killed, either in action or in captivity. Three more were wounded before they could start work; and twenty-three survived arrest and imprisonment. (Foot. op.cit.) We will find out later what happened to the women agents sent in.

Shortly after Thompson joined the Belgian Section, he said that when Mr. Duff-Torrance took over from Mr.

Dadson, Major Claude Knight was in command of the Belgian Section, Captain Jocelyn Clarke ran the Operations sub-section and, from November 1941, Captain, later Lieutenant Colonel, Hardy Amies, ran the recruiting and training sub-section.

Amies was a fashion designer and had previously lived and worked in Germany. Fluent in German and proficient in French, he joined the Intelligence Service when war broke out and worked for the SOE, training agents at Beaulieu to identify the uniforms of the different German military personnel. Many agents commented on how finely dressed he was. His uniform was made for him by a high class tailor in Savile Row and on his sleeve he wore his parachute wings, awarded after three drops at Ringway. On one of the memos in his file is a list of Belgian agents with Shakespearean code-names on which he had written, *'What a wonderful cast. May I do the costumes?'* ('Hardy Amies: Operation Ratweek, Secret War, Athena Learning DVD, Episode 2, (2011) The training report in his personnel file included a comment that, "*This officer is far tougher both physically and mentally than his rather precious appearance would suggest.*" (Ibid.) After the war he become Queen Elizabeth's favourite fashion designer.

As the work Thompson was doing with cover stories, documents, operational clothing and equipment became more onerous, he was provided with a French-speaking Personal Assistant, to whom he was able to dictate his agents' cover stories. She was Marie Koslowska (née Lee-Graham), the wife of an English officer.

> *I never lived to regret it, for she was just what I needed. She was brought up in France (I am not certain that she was not partially of French ancestry) and some of my Belgian colleagues claimed that she spoke better and purer French than he did. She had a flair for Cover Story work, and entered into it with enthusiasm. She was exceptionally good with our agents, looking after their welfare and comfort in*

every way, and they were all very fond of her. In addition she had great patience and skill in interrogation of returning agents (on living conditions etc in Belgium). (www.thompsononename.org.uk/pdf/SOE.pdf 27 June 2009)

Maybe our four women passed through their hands. Why were there so few women sent to Belgium when over fifty were sent into France? Thompson, who was transferred in 1943, said that *"In at least one other Country Section I believe that women were used very successfully, but not in our Section, possibly for lack of suitable material."* Elaine, Olga and Frédérique were sent in very late in the war to act as couriers, liaising between agents already in the field and members of the resistance as well as arranging for messages and reports to be coded and sent back to London. When the anonymous blond was sent it is undocumented.

The Courier cannot be classified as any particular type of individual. He could be highly educated or a working peasant. Possibly the main assets for a Courier are to be completely unobtrusive, to be "unlikely", to have a detailed knowledge of the terrain, and to have an innate skill and cunning in avoiding controls, crossing frontiers and inter-zonal border lines. A high standard of honesty was also needed, since sometimes very large sums of money were carried. (Ibid.)

Elaine Madden

The Comète line website mentioned that 21-year-old Elaine Madden, later known as Elaine Blaize, codenamed *Alice,* was the only female Belgian agent sent into Belgium. She was parachuted into a field near Beauraing, a small town south of Namur on 3/4 August 1944 as part of operation MANDAMUS. Accompanying her were 29-year-old Major André Wendelen and 21-year-old Jacques van de Spiegle,

She was to act as Wendelen's courier on what was his third mission. He had been in the Belgian Carabiniers until early 1940, when ill-health forced him to retire and start a career as a lawyer. In May, he fled to France and was helped to reach England by a Polish escape line. On being interrogated at the Patriotic School, he was recruited into the SOE in July 1941.

According to Foot, Roger de Wesselow, the commanding officer at Wanborough Manor, SOE's preliminary school, thought highly of Wendelen. At Arisaig he was judged first class and his instructor on the Lysander course found him flawless. One of T Sections stars, he was later described as their most distinguished agent. (Foot, op.cit.p.278)

His first mission on 28 January 1942 was to liaise with Group G, a resistance network set up the Cercle du Libre Examen at the Université Libre de Bruxelles. On collecting important intelligence about the situation in Belgium and helping with propaganda and electrical sabotage, he returned to England down the escape line. On 11/12 August 1943, codenamed Tybalt, he and Jacques Doneux, his radio operator, codenamed Hillcat, were parachuted back to contact 'Socrates', the codename of Raymond Scheyven. A young director of Banque Allard and financial genius, 'Socrates' had built up a nation-wide organisation for the distribution of funds to the many Resistance groups operating under SOE's control. Once Wendelen's mission was completed, he used the Comète line to return to England. (Johns, P. *Within Two Cloak,s,* William Kimber, p.158)

Foot's research stated that this was his third trip, with a mission to locate Prince Charles and, with Elaine's assistance, bring him back to England. However, other sources tell a different story.

Lieven Saerens of CEGESOMA, the Centre for Historical Research and Documentation on War and Contemporary Society in Belgium, told me that, according to Elaine's extensive dossier in the Belgian

State Security, she was born in Poperinge on 7 May 1923 to Harold Madden, an English publican, and Caroline Duponselle. When her mother died in childbirth ten years later, her father remarried and worked as a gardener at the war graves in Ypres. Elaine was sent to live with her grandparents and, as a clever, popular and attractive teenager, became a prefect at the Eton Memorial School in Ypres, funded by Eton students in memory of the 342 Etonians who lost their lives fighting in the First World War. (Email communication with John Clinch of belgiumww2 website)

When Elaine left school, she started training as a nurse but, following the German invasion, the War Graves Commission ordered its gardeners at Ypres to evacuate with their families. The situation was serious. Only a few days after her seventeenth birthday, a note in her personnel file in the National Archives, described how,

> *At about noon on the 17th May 1940 after the first air-raid on Paperinghe (sic) I walked down the Rue de l'Hôpital with my aunt named Simone. There was considerable damage everywhere and the services responsible had not yet had time to clear away bodies that were scattered about in the streets. We hadn't walked 100 yards when we saw the head of a man lying in the gutter. Although gruesome it was a fascinating sight and one that neither of use will ever forget. We stopped for quite a few minutes and stared not being able to believe our eyes and then walked away feeling slightly sick and dazed. From there we went on up the Rue de l'Hôpital and turned right down the road to the house another Aunt named Antoinette occupied. We stayed there until about 6 p.m. and made our way back home. The streets had been cleared by this time and there were no further incidents.* (TNA HS 6/112)

The following day, 250 men, women and children, gathered in the school playground with commandeered bicycles, cars and buses to begin a nightmarish expedition to Calais.

When her grandparents heard of this, they told Elaine that she would be safer in England and told her to join them. Accompanied by her 19-year-old aunt Simone, they cycled south down roads crowded with escaping refugees being strafed and bombed by German Stuka planes.

After several days sleeping rough in meadows, they eventually caught up with the tail end of the retreating Expeditionary Forces. Elaine showed them her British papers and begged a lift from soldiers on a British lorry heading for Dunkirk. One of them told her that he had a daughter her age and could not bear to leave her there as she was British. As he knew they were not to take civilians, he told her and her aunt to put on a tin helmet, put their hair up, wear a greatcoat and to just sit there, not to move and not to show their faces. It was a tortuous journey over bomb craters, flooded fields and roads strewn with bodies. When they eventually got to Dunkirk, just before midnight, the whole town was ablaze. (Elliot, S. and Fox, J. *The Children who Fought Hitler,* John Murray, 2009)

Masquerading as soldiers, Elaine and an estimated 330,000 others were rescued by the 'little ships' that had rushed to Dunkirk to evacuate the stranded Expeditionary Force. '*It was a terrifying place. We stood for countless hours on a wooden pier with queues of soldiers,*' she recalled. '*It was like sleepwalking- we slowly shuffled forward with all these flames around us and bombers coming overhead.*' (*The Daily Mail,* 'The Children who fought Hitler: How British ex-pats became the Third Reich's fiercest foes' Lisa Sewards, 23 October 2009)

After hours of waiting, they eventually climbed down a rope ladder into a trawler, where a sharp-eyed officer noticed the young women's ankles. They had not been provided with military trousers. It did not matter. They were safe.

Arriving in England on 1 June 1940, just as the Blitz was starting, she continued her studies at St Ellen's College, London before being called up to work for the ATS, the Auxiliary Transport Service. However, fluent in three languages and with a good knowledge of Belgium, she was transferred to the Belgian section of the SOE. Her job was a *"comptable steno-dactylo"* for Major Ides Floor, a Belgian businessman who had been working in London for a year and a friend of General Colin Gubbins, the Head of SOE. After six months in Gibraltar, Floor had been appointed the liaison officer at the Belgian State Security, 32 Chapel Street, London, W.1. What happened to her aunt Simone has not come to light. (Elliot, S. and Fox, J. op.cit.)

In her personnel file in the National Archives is a report on her mission, codenamed IMOGEN. The name on the earliest forms, dated 8 May 1944, almost three months before she was parachuted back into Belgium, stated that she was E. Meeus, presumably her cover name whilst she underwent SOE training. The name on the forged identity card was Hélène Marie Maes, issued by the Belgian office in Nice. There were salary receipts and a residence permit for an apartment in Paris owned by a Mme Dervaux. Her papers told her that, before she left, she would be given a 'Gestapo' style interrogation to discover whether her cover story had any weaknesses.

She was told she would be provided with appropriate clothing and toiletries for the three months she would be in Belgium and given whatever 'equipment' she thought suitable for her parachute jump and landing. Details were provided for her return trip to England once her mission had been completed and there were pages of coding that she had to master with the help of Captain Whittaker.

Annexe "K" in her personnel file provided fascinating details of the coding system being used in the run up to D-Day. On 31st May 1944, whilst she was at the Vineyard (S.T.S. 35), one of SOE' requisitioned houses in the grounds of Beaulieu, she met with a Captain Whittaker. He went through the codes she had to use when communicating with HQ from the field.

The Cipher being used was Playfair Rimmer with the Keyword BAYSWATER. Playfair was a simple substation code on a 25-letter word square. See if you're as bright as she was. The special arrangements included suppressing the letter "Z", CH had to be used for K, EX for X, IN for Y and . . EZ for Z. Numbers one to ten were their equivalent letters in the alphabet. The "dud" letter used for null was X. The security check in case she was compromised was to have twenty-one words in the first sentence. The code was to start at the first word in the third sentence. The interval between 'pregnant' words had to be every fifth and the code was to end at the last exclamation mark. Courtesy forms at the beginning and end were to be ignored, apostrophes and hyphens were both 1 and the specimen cage of a square was:

```
BAYSW
TERCD
FGHIJ
KLMNO
PQUVX
```

Having mastered that, in a document dated 27 July 1944, a week before her flight, she was provided with her codes. See whether you can get your head round them. She was informed that the prefix for all her incoming messages was 578 and for her outgoing ones 195. The T.15 check was that 1 and 2 were to be added on the third and fourth and that "E" would be used for dead letters. Annexe "J" included her MENTAL ONE-TIME PAD PLUS MENTAL INDICATOR with the remark that the substitution square letter was "Y".

A	SEQUESTERED	N	SAVETHE
A	CONTINUOUS	N	OTHER
B	FROM	O	SACRED
B	POUNDING	O	ALLIED
C	THIS	P	MONUMENTS
C	OFENEMY	P	AIRCRAFT
D	NOISY	Q	OVER

Return to Belgium

D	TARGETS	Q	HAS
E	WORLD	R	WHICH
E	BY	R	SOFAR
F	COULDI	S	THE
F	LIBERATORS	S	PROVED
G	WEAR	T	WINGS
G	FORTRESSES	T	VERY
H	OUT	U	OF
H	MOSQUITOES	U	SUCCESSFUL
I	THIS	V	CENTURIES
I	MARAUDERS	V	MANY
J	TRANSITORY	W	HAVE
J	THUNDERBOLTS	W	FACTORIES
K	BEINGIN	X	SILENTLY
K	MUSTANGS	X	HAVE
L	PEACEFUL	Y	PASSED
L	LIGHTNINGS	Y	BEEN
M	CONTEMPLATION	Z	BY
M	AND	Z	DESTROYED

POEM FOR MENTAL INDICATOR

A	RESISTANCE	N	SETBY
B	CONTINUES	O	THEIR
C	MEN	P	BRILLIANT
D	WORK	Q	AND
E	INDEPENDENTLY	R	COURAGEOUS
F	ORWITH	S	LEADERS
G	ORGANIZATIONS	T	PROPITIOUS
H	FOLLOWING	U	HEAVEN
I	THE	V	MUST
J	GREAT	W	SURELY
K	AND	X	SAVE
L	INSPIRING	Y	THESE
M	EXAMPLES	Z	HEROES

(Ibid.)

The code word she had to use with the above poem was WORLD. Her true check in every message was the fifth letter indicator chosen by the Mental Indicator System. Just in case she was transmitting under duress she was given a bluff check which was: "7th letter of message increased by alphabetical equivalent of number of message gives 1st letter of 7th word." The Mental Indicators were prefixed with the keyword – WORLD.

NTRGP   IKFEO   ENTRE   HGRUE   FERCL

FOTSA	PHLMN	CDAPB	TASGI	TLSHD
SZUYC	FEWIR	TMIGN	DINPO	AFTVE
SOJIR	IENAG	HOTER	EABLS	XTSOU
LDFEN	SRTLO	PEOIN	IEODP	WOLMU
HILWN	ATONS	RENAS	POEQN	VIESU
IEHNR	FYIAE	UTRDS	UIEVT	BSTVA

(Ibid.)

Do you understand that? Good. The SOE advisers showed advanced planning and foresight. She was given an address in Basle in Switzerland for any 'innocent' letters she might want to write. In them she had refer to herself as Marie Antoinette, use one if 'the address was her safe house', two if 'the first has been cancelled, here is my new one', three for 'I am in my safe house, come and find me' and four for 'I am going to Nancy'. The signature she was to use was Barnabe.

Letters concerning her return to England had to be sent to either an address in Seville, Spain, or one in Lisbon, Portugal. These had to be learned off by heart. Her password in Nancy was : "*Je cherche le bougniat*" and the reply would be "*Vous voulez dire le marchand de charbon.*" Once in Spain her name would be Miss Mary Townsend and, if she got out via Switzerland, she had to ask for Mr. Bateman at the British Embassy.

To be sure she understood the danger of her mission, she was informed that she would be paid as a third class agent and, in the case of her death, her salary would continue being paid into her account for the next six months.

She was provided with 5,000 Belgian Francs to carry on her person but, hidden in a box of talcum powder, were a further 50,000 Belgian francs for her mission and 10,000 French Francs for her return. To put this sum into perspective, Foot said that, by 1943, the SOE was sending ten million Belgium francs' worth of US dollars into Belgium every month. The organisers were expected to convert them into local currency on the black market.

The One-Time-Pad was hidden in her wallet along with microfilms of questionnaires she had to encourage Belgian sympathisers to fill in. Six identity photographs were hidden in a secret pocket. Her valise and the wireless set to be used by *Donalbain* (Jacques Van de Spiegle), the radio operator who would accompany her, were to be dropped with them when they parachuted in.

The date of her flight was not specified in her file, nor was the airfield, but she was told it would be one night during the moon period between 30 July and 12 August 1944. Fernand Strubbe in *"Services Secrets Belges 1940 – 1945"* indicated it was on the night of 3/4 August. The approach to Belgium by RAF pilots had to be taken with great care. The coastal defences of the Atlantik Wall, radar stations, night-fighter bases and light and heavy anti-aircraft guns had been carefully studied so that the safest entry was through a gap in the flak defences at Le Crotoy, at the mouth of the River Somme.

In an interview after the war, reported by Lisa Sewards, Elaine told how she did not have time to think before she did her parachute jump. The American airman opened the hatch, kissed her, picked her up by her harness straps and just dropped her through the hole. (*The Daily Mail,* 'The Children who fought Hitler: How British ex-pats became the Third Reich's fiercest foes' Lisa Sewards, 23 October 2009)

Documents in her file, dated 22 November 1944, six weeks after the Allies invaded Belgium, showed that she made a perfect landing at 0130 hours 7½ kms SSE of Houyet and 3½ kms NE of Pondrome and rendezvoused as instructed at 'Ferme du Fisique' without any mishap. It was situated on the crossroads of two farm tracks on the edge of Chy Wood. The password she had to use was "*Je viens chercher le kilo de Café emballé dans la serviette et apporter de quoi faire use nouvelle bride pour l'étalon.*" She was told that Tybalt (one of Wendelen's codenames), had already left the coffee with the farmer and warned that she had not got to take the train to Martouz-in-Neuville. "*Le chef de gare est Rexiste et dangereux.*"

Donalbain, her wireless operator, was to be known in Belgium as *Foxtrot*. Her codename in Belgium was to be *Alice* and Wendelen, her 'Chef de Mission', was codenamed *Brabantio* but known in Belgium as *Odette*. The password she had to use with him was *"Je viens chercher Mlle Olive Chartres"* and the response had to be *"Vous voulez dire la cousine de Georges"*. In case additional proof of her identity was needed, she was told that a personal message *"Nous irons cueillir les murons"* would be broadcast at 1915 hours on Radio Belgium for the first three days after her arrival and repeated on the twelfth.

Odette was to put her in contact with *Huguette*, another SOE agent who would been parachuted into Belgium in May 1944 to co-ordinate sabotage of the railway network. Philippe Connart told me that Huguette was 29-year old Baron Jules Rolin, an artillery reserve officer, also known as *Messala* and *Ridder*. The MESSALA file in the National Archives added that Huguette was also to replace *Nelly* and organise sabotage groups.

Research on the dbnl website showed that *Nelly* was Jules Guillery, who, before Rolin, led a committee made up of the Secret Army, Group G, the Belgian National Movement and the Partisans of the Opposition. According to the VERGILLIA file in the National Archives, in February 1944, he was sent out from Tempsford as chief of a sabotage organisation under the command of the Chiefs of Staff, SOE and the Belgian Sûreté, with the aim of dislocating rail and road transportation on D-Day.

Following the D-Day landings in Normandy in June, the next targets for the Allies were the capture of Paris and the liberation of Belgium. Group G successfully sabotaged the country's railway and canal system, forcing German reinforcements a week's delay in getting to Normandy. This gave Elaine's mission a particular importance but also imposed strict limits on it. What she was warned about was the need for strict discipline. Her briefing notes told her:

> *1. You are going to find yourself amongst people who have resisted magnificently an unprecedented oppression. This will make you ask yourself some*

questions, to suggest potential contacts, to offer you some actions that haven't been foreseen in your mission. It is an exceptionally dangerous situation, one in which you must not put yourself at any risk. The essential condition amongst all these operations is security and everyone must accomplish their tasks to the best of their ability.
    2. You have to avoid engaging the Belgian government or the British authorities in the field of politics. Every initiative in this mission has the possibility of creating a dangerous confusion in the actions and plans of the War Cabinet.
    3. The duty of ambassadors like you is to be especially focussed on quiet reserve and to use the utmost discretion as an observer, concerned with your own mission and its planning. Knowledge of both the British and Belgian points of view needs to be at its heart. (TNA HS 6/112)

    Her plan of action was to follow SHAEF's aims and objectives. The first was to slow down the arrival of enemy troops before they could engage the invasion forces, in particular their artillery units, tanks and armoured cars. The second was to slow down the placement of reinforcements in areas near the Allies' bridgeheads. The third was to hinder German aerial attacks on Allied troops. The fourth was to hinder river transport and the last was to transmit back to London all information about military matters, no matter how great or small.
    She was instructed to inform HUGUETTE, SOE's main organiser, who would execute SHAEF's orders. As his courier, she would be the go-between between him, SHAEF and the different resistance groups. To pass on messages she had to use HUGUETTE's existing contacts. Any personal contact she might have with the chiefs of the resistance groups had to be kept to an absolute minimum. Her security had not to be put in danger. The individuality of the resistance groups had to be respected and, where possible, given autonomy in

carrying out appropriate action.

The principal groups she was told she would be working with were the Front de l'Indépendance, Group G, Group Nola and the Mouvement National Belge. In the section headed GENERAL NOTES she was told that the group targeting the railways had to immobilise rail transport. Another had to cut all telephone communications by bringing down pylons, cutting telephone cables and attacking Brussels' central telephone exchange.

She had to insist that none of the groups had overall control of discipline. Their orders had to come through SHAEF which included target for sabotage.

> *The Allied Command wishes concentrated coordinated attacks to be made on the following types of target when special Action Signals are given:*
>
> *<u>Railways:</u> Action against the railways will consist of:*
>
> *a) The elimination of key enemy personnel brought from Germany to control military transport by rail.*
>
> *b) The destruction of railway lines by the use of explosives or, if sufficient time and personnel are available, by the removal of lengths of rail.*
>
> *c) The destruction of breakdown trains.*
>
> *d) The interruption and disorganisation of railway telephone and signals systems by the cutting of lines, destruction of cabins, etc.*
>
> *e) Destruction of railway turntables.*
>
> *f) <u>Light</u> destruction of the railway watering system, e.g. by cutting of mains.*
>
> *<u>General Note</u>: Complicated or heavy installations which would require more than a week to repair should not be destroyed, but should be sabotaged by having their essential parts removed. These parts should be kept carefully and placed at the disposal of the Allied Forces on their arrival. It should be born in mind that as a general rule the continuity of railway*

dislocation must depend on the repetition of the derailments and light sabotage, rather than on massive destruction.

    Enemy Road Movements. It is certain that the enemy will use the roads for the massive transport of troops and equipment when invasion takes place. Every effort should be made to sabotage such movements, e.g. by improvised road blocks; displacement of traffic signs; setting of booby traps; placing of small mines. Such action should be entirely clandestine, and no risk should be taken of being involved in pitched battles with enemy effectives.

    2. Telecommunications. The cutting of telephone and telegraph lines and cables (preferably undetectably) and the removal and safe-keeping of essential parts of such installations. Installations of this kind, even in cases whether have been requisitioned by the enemy, are not to be destroyed but only lightly sabotaged.

    2. Waterways. Dislocation of communications by inland waterways, e.g. by the destruction of lock gates; and by the sabotage of enemy munitions shipments.

    3. Air Targets. Sabotage of enemy aircraft; airfield installations; light repair plant and aviation fuel dumps, particularly in the area between Courtrai/Ghent and the coast. Enemy flying personnel should be sniped where occasion presents itself, without the risk of becoming engaged in a stand-up fight with the enemy. (Ibid.)

A note at the end of this list pointed out that the procedure regarding action signals was known to NELLY and HUGUETTE. Foot identified nine civilian resistance groups with military names in Belgium. The largest was Front de l'lindépendence et Libération which had two subsidiaries, the Partisans and the Armée de Milice Patriotique. There were also the Movement National Belge, the Organisation Militaire Belge de Résistance

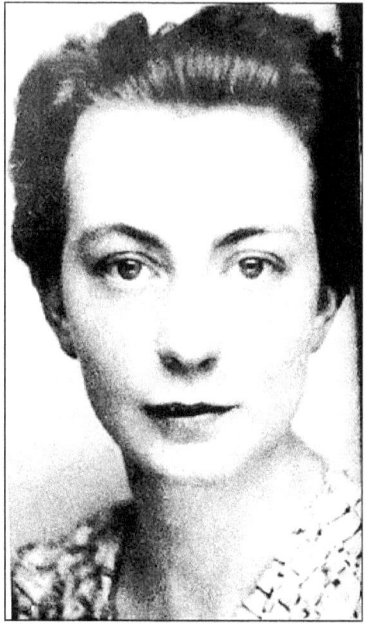

Andrée De Jongh

Took over the role of organising the Comète line in 1941 after Henri de Bliqui and Arnold Deppé were arrested. Only 24 and working as a commercial artist, she nursed wounded troops and then arranged for hundreds of Belgian and British soldiers and downed aircrews to escape from Belgium and France into Spain and then back to England via Gibraltar or Lisbon. Supported by the Airey Neave, her SIS controller, in London. Her father, Frederic, took over after she was betrayed by an informer in January 1943. She was arrested and interrogated but the Gestapo did not believe her admission that she was the organiser. Survived Ravensbrück and Mauthausen concentration camps.. http://www.truenorthperspective.com/24104.jpg
19th July 2009)

Baron Jacques Donny

Director of Sofina company employing Andrée De Jongh. Financed and supported her trip to Spain in August 1941. Captured and imprisoned. Shot in Stuttgart 29th February 1944

(http://home.clara.net/clinchy/cometeph.htm 19th July 2009)

Gérard Waucquez

Brussels industrialist given various diplomatic missions including escorting Captain Woolton, General Haig's grandson, into Spain and delivering important military information to the Belgian government-in-exile in London. After SOE training, sent from RAF Tempsford and parachuted into a farm in Marchiennes, near St-Amand-les-Eaux in northern France with funds for various Resistance networks, some underground presses and orders for the escape of the André De Staercke, wanted by Premier Pierlot to be Chef de Cabinet, and Fernand Spaak, the son of Minister of Foreign Affairs. Betrayed and sentenced to death, he was imprisoned in Essen, Veckta and Kaisem before being liberated by the Americans in April 1945. (www.praats.be/comete.htm 19th July 2009)

Return to Belgium

Baron Robert Goffinet

Aide de camp of Prince Charles, brother of King Léopold III. Lost his eye fighting in First World War. Tried to help royal family join government-in-exile but they refused. Funded resistance and passed on vital military information to his family friend, Gérard Waucquez, to take to England. Accompanied Prince Charles whilst he was in hiding during the war in Sart-lez-Spa.

(http://www.cometeline.org/ABChelpers.html 19th July 2009)

The War Office, Whitehall, London. Here Airey Neave and Jimmy Langley of MI9 shared Room 300, where they planned the support of the Comète and other escape lines.

(http://upload.wikimedia.org/wikipedia/commons/7/7f/Old_war_office.jpg 27th October 2009)

Norgeby House, 83 Baker Street, London, where SOE's Belgian Section had three rooms for their Headquarters from 1941-45.
Their civilian secretaries had another room.

www.bca.uk.com/viewcentre.aspx?cid=983 27th October 2009

Winterfold, Cranleigh, Surrey, (STS 4) where potential Belgian agents were assessed as to their suitability for clandestine activity.

(Courtesy of Steven Kippax)

Arisaig House, Inverness-shire, Northwest Scotland, one of the secluded country houses where Belgian and other agents were trained in the art of 'ungentlemanly warfare'.

http://i466.photobucket.com/albums/rr29/ianj2008/DSC01150.jpg
12th November 2009

Dunham House, Cheshire, where Belgian and other agents were accommodated whilst they had their parachute training at nearby Ringway airport, near Manchester.

http://farm1.static.flickr.com/12/16413226_857f970399.jpg 24th August 2009

Beaulieu Abbey, Hampshire, SOE's 'Finishing School' where Belgian and other agents were given intensive training in clandestine operations. They were accommodated in large houses within the grounds of the estate.

http://koti.welho.com/rhurmal1/linnat2004/img0007.jpg 24th August 2009

Return to Belgium

Arnold Deppé

Film technician who worked with Andrée de Jongh..
Established Comète line with Henri de Bliqui.
Accompanied escaped Belgian soldiers and British
prisoners through France and into Spain. Captured in
Lille in August 1941. Tortured without results, he was
sentenced to death and imprisoned at Rheinbach,
Mauthausen, Natzweiler-Struthof and Dachau from
where he was liberated by the Americans in May
1945.

(http://www.comete-bidassoa.com/images/Arn_Deppe.jpg 29th October 2009)

André Wendelen

Brussels lawyer. Escaped to England and joined SOE. Trained in sabotage, flew on three missions from RAF Tempsford, the last on 3/4th August 1944. Parachuted with Elaine Madden and Jacques van de Spiegle near Beauraing.

(http://www.praats.be/socrates.htm
27th October 2009)

Return to Belgium

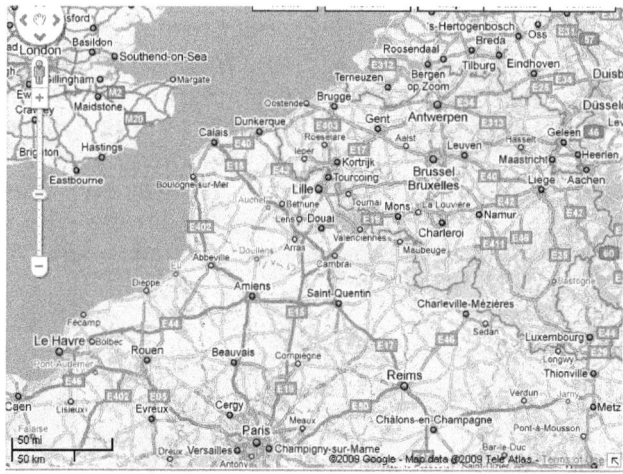

Extracts of Googlemaps showing the route of the Comète Line along which many hundreds of people were escorted from Belgium, through France into Spain and eventually back to England via Gibraltar or Lisbon.

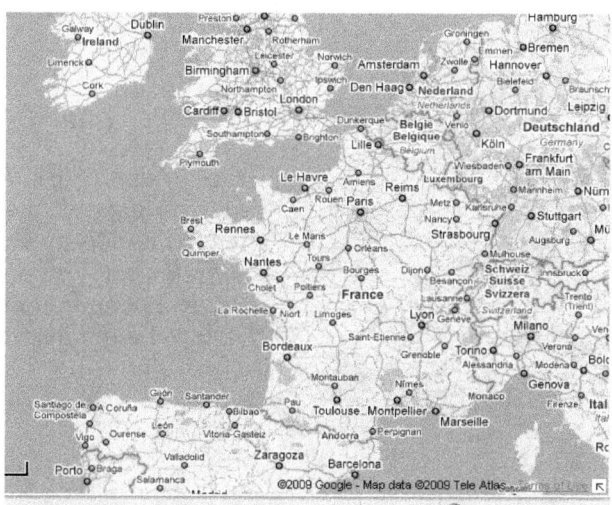

Extract of a photograph of Elaine Madden and her Aunt Simone safely arrived in Britain after the evacuation of Dunkirk in May/June 1940. (From an unnamed British newspaper article 'Shapely ankles gave girls away'.)

Extract of a photograph of Elaine after being called up to join the Auxiliary Transport Service . (From 'The Children who Fought Hitler' TV documentary.)

Photograph of Elaine's identity papers given to her in London by the SOE. (From 'The Children who Fought Hitler' TV documentary)

Return to Belgium

Andrée de Jongh and her father Frédéric

Headmaster who helped provide safe houses in Brussels for escaped prisoners-of-war and wounded soldiers. Took over the organising of the Comète line after Andrèe was arrested. He was captured in June 1943 and executed in March 1944.

(http://home.clara.net/clinchy/bulletin.htm 23rd August 2009)

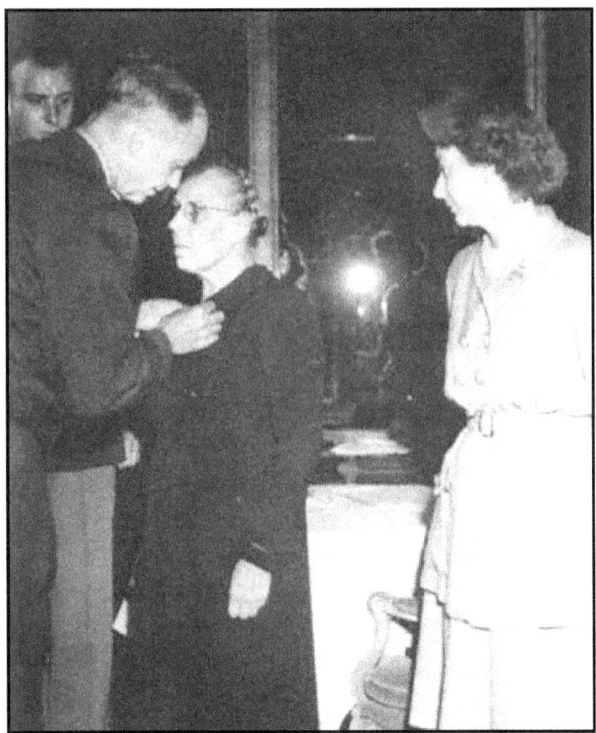

Marie Louise Dissard and Andrée De Jongh

Both women were awarded the American Medal of Freedom after the war. They had both taken over the running of the PAT and Comète lines when their respective organisers had been captured. Between them, they helped over a thousand people get out of Belgium and France and back to England.

(http://www.spartacus.schoolnet.co.uk/FRdissard.htm 23rd August 2009)

Elaine Madden

Born in Poperinge in 1923, she escaped from Dunkirk in May 1940 dressed as a soldier. Trained as a secretary in London, she worked in Belgian State Security. Recruited by SOE in January 1944 she failed her Morse course but was trained as a courier. Flown out on 4th August 1944, probably from RAF Tempsford by 138 Squadron, she was parachuted into Belgium on Operation Brabantio.

(Courtesy of Philippe Connart)

HRH Prince Charles of Belgium

(alias Monsieur Jules Bernard) Anglophile brother of King Léopold III. Belgian government-in-exile and SOE planned to 'lift him out' in August 1944 in case he was captured by Germans. Part of Elaine's mission was to organise his evacuation from hiding at Sart-lez-Spa after the King had been deported.

(http://www.thepeerage.com/101763_001.jpg 23rd August 2009)

Return to Belgium

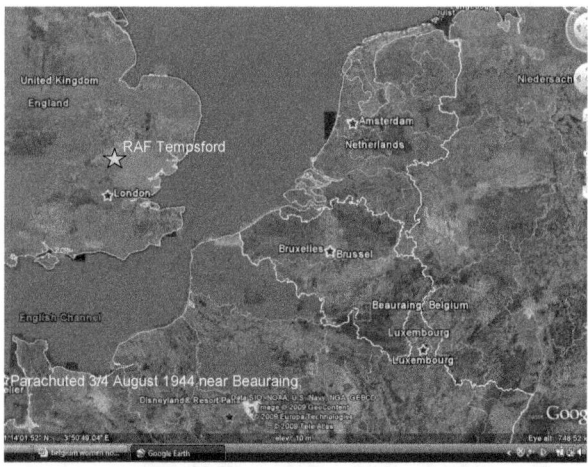

Extracts from Googlemaps showing the location of Elaine Madden's drop zone near Beauraing and the Chateau in Halloy where Prince Charles and Baron Goffinet were staying.

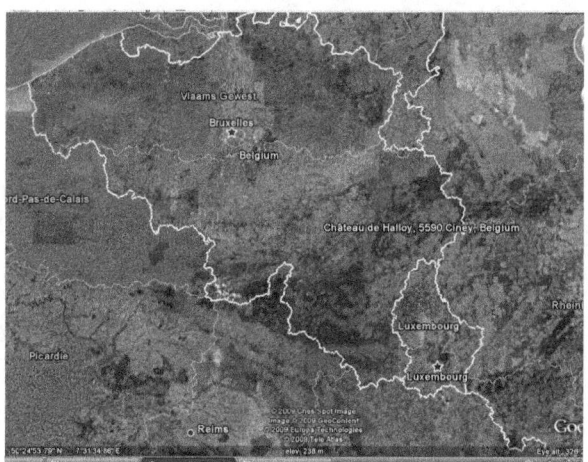

Airey Neave

MI9's coordinator of escape and evasion organisation, helped finance and support Andrée de Jongh's Cométe line.

http://www.tremele.nl/Oorlog/wo2/05regimenten/
LeoHeaps/AireyNeave_young.jpg

Return to Belgium

Hardy Amies,

Head of SOE's 'T' Section (Belgium) and later dressmaker for Queen Elizabeth II.

http://easyandelegantlife.com/wp-content/uploads/2009/02/hardyamies.jpg

Major Graham T.R. Thompson

Worked in SOE's Belgian Section and wrote about his wartime experiences in *'SOE in Belgium'*.

(http://uk.groups.yahoo.com/group/specialoperationsexecutive/
photos/album/171075687/pic/1179305673/view?
picmode=&mode=tn&order=ordinal&start=1&count=20&dir=asc)

Return to Belgium

CHÂTEAU DE HALLOY
Ardennes, Belgium where in August/September 1944 Elaine met Monsieur Jules Bernard (Prince Charles, son of King Leopold II). Her mission was to locate an airfield from where a Lysander could fly him back to Britain.
www.chateaudehalloy.be/default.asp?langid=33

Extract from Googlemaps showing the Chateau at Halloy and the airstrip at Sovet. Elaine's radio operator was lodged nearby but when the owner was arrested and German railway workers installed, communication with London was a problem.

Frédérique Dupuich

Born in Brussels in 1900 ,she worked as a secretary and did some nursing. Got involved in Resistance work. Escaped when friends were arrested by accompanying nine Belgian individuals with Arnold Deppé and Andrée De Jongh down Comète line into Spain. Got back to England and worked in the Belgian State Security. Appointed to secretary and assistant of the section head of the Political Warfare and Propaganda Department. Joined SOE in 1944, trained, and, after many delays, was sent by Lysander to France to liaise with various networks. Arrested, survived interrogation and met American 9th Army in Brittany.

(Courtesy of Philippe Connart)

Olga Jackson (née Thioux)

No photo of Olga has come to light. She got out of Belgium before the war broke out. What she did in England is unknown but she was recruited by the SOE and, after training, was thought to have been flown out of RAF Tempsford and parachuted near Ledeberg on 3/4th August 1944. Hers was a propaganda mission, aimed at demoralising German officers through prostitution, drugs and alcohol so they would be less of a threat when the Allies invaded Belgium on 2nd September. She was 37.

Halifax DG245 of 138 Squadron, RAF Tempsford. A hole was cut in the bottom of the fuselage to allow containers and parachutists to be dropped into Belgium and other countries in occupied Europe.

(In Freddy Clark's *Agents by Moonlight* courtesy of P.R.O. Kew)

Westland Lysander used to take and pick up agents and VIPs from Tempsford (and RAF Tangmere on south coast). Note the ladder attached to the fuselage to allow passengers quicker access and the additional fuel tank to increase its range.
(www.jaapteeuwen.com/.../westland%20lysander.jpg 24th August 2009)

View approaching RAF Tempsford from the south.
October 13th 1942
(Courtesy of RAF Museum, Hendon)

Aerial photograph of RAF Tempsford 1943. It was designed by an illusionist to give the appearance that it was a disused airfield. Agents sent into Belgium and other destinations in occupied Europe were flown from here.
(Courtesy of Harrington Aviation Museum)

Gibraltar Farm, Tempsford Airfield, Bedfordshire, the nerve centre of SOE's TOP SECRET airfield. Hitler is said to have called it a viper's nest but it was never attacked throughout the war. Agents were given their final briefing in the farmhouse.

http://www.wartimememories.co.uk/airfields/GibralterFarm-1.jpg 29th October 2009

The barn, all that remains of Gibraltar Farm. It was in here where Belgian and other agents were checked by an RAF officer to ensure they had no incriminating items on their person. They were kitted out with parachute, harness, helmet, gloves, ankle supports, boots, and a choice of dagger or revolver, a flask of whisky, rum or brandy and a choice of pills—one of which was cyanide.

(Courtesy of John Button)

Return to Belgium

Inside of the barn showing the concrete shelving on which parachutes, harnesses and other supplies for the agents were stored. It is now a memorial to the brave deeds of the men and women of every nationality who left for their missions from here.

(Courtesy of Bernard O'Connor)

The Control Tower or "Watchtower' of Tempsford Airfield. Its codename was BRASSTRAY.
(http://www.deborahjackson.net/assets/images/
timemeddlers2_tempsford 29th October 2009)

Idesbald Floor, Hardy Amies, Badouin de Borchgrave d'Altena and Georges Aronstein, officers in charge of SOE's Belgian section during the war.
(Courtesy of Philippe Connart)

Chicheley Park, Newport Pagnell, Buckinghamshire, where, from 1940—1942, Belgian agents were housed before being sent on missions by the Special Duties Squadrons.
http://farm4.static.flickr.com/3070/2610352907_3866e226ca_o.jpg
27th October 2009

Audley End House, Essex, where, early in the war, some Belgian and other agents were accommodated before being driven to Newmarket racecourse for their flight into Europe.
(http://www.grouptravelorganiser.com/assets/8/7/
Audleyend_fullsize.jpg 23rd August 2009)

Gaynes Hall, Cambridgeshire, where, from 1942–1944, Belgian and other agents were accommodated prior to being driven to RAF Tempsford or RAF Harrington for their missions.
(http://upload.wikimedia.org/wikipedia/en/5/5f/Gaynes_Hall_tmb.jpg
23rd August 2009)

and the Armée de Libération as well as three groups devoted to sabotage: Group G, Hotton and Nola. There were also a number of escape lines. (Foot, op.cit. p.241)

Action signals were the coded instructions to the leader of these resistance groups to commence their designated activities. They were to be broadcast by the BBC in their *'messages personnels'* after the 1900 hours Belgian news. All the information she collected had to be forwarded to London taking into account the fact that the expression 'large bodies of troops' meant units of approximately 500 men or more, and included concentrations, which could not easily be seen from the air, e.g. bivouacs in woods. Exact grid references were essential. Field post numbers or the divisional signs on vehicles had to be provided. She was informed that wireless aerials and despatch rider activity often indicated the presence of a headquarters, which could then be identified by its pennants or painted signs. Any information about petrol and ammunition dumps would be particularly important, as would any information about rockets, flying bombs and other secret weapon sites. It was urged that her reports had always to include: -

> *a) The date and time of observation, as opposed to the time at which the source may have originated the telegram. It must be clear whether zone time (G.M.T.) or local time is being used.*
>
> *b) A description of the place in sufficient detail to enable it to be pinpointed, in the case of static targets, with a six-figure map reference if possible.*
>
> *In addition, reports should show whether the originator is himself the source; if the report has been received from a third party, the latter's identity or reliability should be stated.*
>
> *These instructions do not affect the original proviso that there is no onus on any agent to send information and that he must never allow the despatch of information to jeopardise his other activities or his security. Nor should vague deductions be made, though reliable indications of*

future moves and negative information are of value. (Ibid.)

The microfilm copies of the questionnaire Elaine was provided with were of particularly interest, revealing not only the extent of the Allies' existing knowledge of Germany's latest weaponry but also their very serious concerns about its use.

1. Information is required as to the methods at present in use for transporting component parts of the flying bombs, its launching trolley, and the materials used for fuelling the bomb and providing rocket propulsion, to the depots where it is stored prior to use.

2. The bomb may be transported in one piece (without planes), in which case the length would be 22 ft. and the diameter about 3 ft. alternatively the war-head may be transported separately; it is a truncated cone of length 47 ins., minimum diameter 28 ins., and maximum diameter 33 ins. The forward end is rounded and the base hollow.

It is required to know if the above parts can be identified as travelling by road or rail, if there are completely crated or merely protected by a skeleton crate, how they are guarded, and if there is any possibility of access during a halt or during marshalling.

3. The launching trolley with the rocket propulsion unit may be transported separately by road or rail.

We want complete details of the trolley, and if possible, a sketch or photograph.

4. At some time prior to launching, the bomb is fuelled with petrol and the rocket propulsion unit on the trolley is filled with hydrogen peroxide,

Where is this done? Probably one filling station serves a number of launching sites.

5. An important constituent of the rocket propulsion fuel is almost certainly hydrogen peroxide. This is stored in 2500 gallon aluminium tanks, which may be above or below ground. The storage tanks are supplied by road or rail. Rail transport may be either (I) by large aluminium tank wagons (length of wagon 60 ft.; tank diameter 8 ft. 6 ins.; tank length 30 ft.) or (ii) by a number (12/14) of small aluminium tanks 4 ft. in diameter and 4 ½ to 5 ft. high, arranged in close contact in a double row.

Is there any evidence of road transport? This may be in carboys of 13 gallons capacity.

In the case of rail transport, we wish to know if there is a wooden floor or other woodwork in the tank wagon construction.

Is there any opportunity of access to the wagons at sidings or marshalling yards?

Is there any opportunity of attacking the wagons by rifle or mortar fire from a distance of say 100 yards?

6. If any depots, assembly or filling points are located, we want to know what kind of road transport is allowed to enter them.

Are any foreign workers allowed to enter?

Are lorries subjected to careful inspection at the entrance?

Is it possible to approach to say within 100 yards of the boundary fence after dark?

Are there any trees or other means of concealment in the vicinity? (Ibid.)

Reminders about her security might have included being told to read a British government publication aimed at service personnel going into Belgium. What follows is part of the advice given to those sent into Norway but the message would have been equally important.

SECURITY NOTE
Now is the time for you to realise that all that you have learned about security during your training at home applies with equal measure to operations overseas…. One of the most important reasons for this is that you have moved and will continue to move

Return to Belgium

into areas which have been occupied by the Enemy for a long time.

The Enemy will spare no pains to leave behind, scattered among the civilian population, agents, saboteurs and propagandists who will be a continued threat to our security.

Their numbers will greatly exceed anything with which we have had to cope in the past – and it will be infinitely more difficult to detect them. Added to this, the Enemy will have prepared channels of communication for the use of his agents, which he may well be able to use long after actual hostilities have ceased.

So there must be no relaxation of security-mindedness and suspicious alertness, even in those areas where the battle has moved on and comparatively peaceful conditions may prevail. In these areas particularly you must be on your guard.

As you have been told so often, personal responsibility is the key-note of good security. ... **Do not forget that more Europeans understand English than is popularly supposed. So be very careful what you say – not only to civilians, but to each other in their hearing.** *You should keep a particular look-out for suspects, and report immediately any cases which you come across ... Pay particular attention to the checking of identity documents and do not hesitate to detain, if necessary by force, any suspicious individuals. Some of these may be disguised as British officers or men; and it is not unlikely that the beautiful spy will come into her own again.*

The dangers of sabotage will also be considerable. This means that when you are guarding material or equipment, your job will be particularly important; and that you must continue to take great care of your personal weapons and equipment.

You must expect that propaganda will be directed to driving a wedge between the Allies, for instance by attempts to promote anti-Russian feeling. There may also be attempts to organise sympathy for the German people. This propaganda, which may be in many forms – some crude and obvious, but some subtle and hard to recognise – will be directed by enemy sympathisers and agents against your morale. Women are clever at this sort of work, and will no doubt often be used. Do not allow yourself to be affected by any of this. You have a job to do – and you must see it through with good will and determination.

Life in ex-German Europe will demand your vigilance, alertness and self-confidence. These must **be used in applying with common sense the security principles you have been taught.**
('Norway', British Government Wartime publication)

The success of operation IMOGEN was not referred to in Elaine's personnel file. We have to presume Elaine managed to pass on SHAEF's directives to the right contacts who acted on them appropriately. However, events changed rapidly and so plans had to be changed.

According to Foot, in April 1944 Jean de Lantsheere of the Nola Group, had managed to get an audience with King Léopold in the gardens of the palace, offering to get him out of the country. As the king's response was that he had chosen to be a prisoner so that he could be of some use to his people, the plan was shelved.

Following the Allied invasion in June, Heinrich Himmler, the head of the Schutzstaffel (SS) and Reichsführer, ordered King Léopold to be deported to a German fort at Hirschstein in Saxony. There were worries about what their plans were for his brother, Prince Charles. According to Strubbe, on 30 July, Jules Rolin, alias *Huguette*, told Albert Delvingt, his radio operator, to encode and transmit a message to London asking them to arrange to exfiltrate the brother of 'patron' de Jean de Lantsheere. This was said to be his last task for the good of the king. A translation of the message in the IMOGEN file reads:

4377/2
FROM MESSALA VIA KINGSTON
30. JULY 1944.
32 MY THIRTY TWO TO THIRTY EIGHT STOP
MOST SECRET STOP
MY RESPONDER JEAN DE LANTSHEERE REPEAT DE LANTSHEERE STOP THE BROTHER OF HIS CHIEF ACTIVELY SEARCHED AFTER BY THE GESTAPO ON ORDERS FROM BERLIN STOP TO FIND HIM HERE WOULD BE DIFFICULT STOP ONLY GOOD SOLUTION DEPARTURE BY AEROPLANE IF IT CAN BE DONE QUICKLY AND WITH THE MINIMUM OF TRAVELLING AND WAITING. STOP REASON FOR THIS PERSON WEAKENED THROUGHT ACUTE SCIATICA STOP WOULD BE ACCOMPANIED STOP I AM THE ONLY ONE AU COURANT. (TNA HS 6/216)

In London, Gubbins and his colleagues in Belgian intelligence understood immediately that Rolin was acting for Prince Charles. The whole matter was politically very sensitive. Rien Emmery of belgiumww2 commented that, over the course of the war, King Léopold had been losing popularity because of his perceived collaboration with the Nazi occupying forces, whilst his brother, the 'anglophile' Charles, increased his. In an attempt to mend the rift between the government-in-exile and the King, they considered bringing Charles back to England. However, some thought it would give the wrong idea because the collaborationist circles in Belgium had "predicted" in a brochure that the Belgian government would try and replace the King with his brother.

On 7 November 1943, Lieutenant Philip Johns took over from Amies as head of SOE's Belgian Section. For the previous two years he had been head of SIS in Lisbon before being transferred for a brief spell in Rio de Janeiro. Johns reported receiving a memo from Charles which read '*Le frère du Patron desire voyager vers la Grand Bretagne. Prier aarranger les moyens du voyage.'* (Johns, op.cit. p.170)

According to the SOE file in the National Archives, Gubbins got the cogs into gear and operation PATRON (SEA) was planned. On a typed page marked TOP SECRET and dated 4 August, the day Elaine arrived in Belgium, Major Ivor Dobson, who had replaced Bingham as head of the Dutch section, wrote to Rear Admiral A. H. Taylor, responsible for SOE's naval operations, with a copy to T Section:

> *Reference our conversation this morning; I would appreciate your passing on this confirmation to Captain SLOCUM, as promised.*
>
> *We have been considering the exfiltration of a high personage from Belgium and the possibility of a Lysander pick-up has been examined.*
>
> *It is my opinion that such an operation even it is found feasible, could not be laid on this moon, which would automatically mean our waiting until the August/September moon commencing in over 3 weeks' time. As the high personage in question is being actively hunted by the Gestapo, a 3 weeks' delay might easily be fatal, and I am consequently anxious for a sea operation to be considered as a possible alternative.*
>
> *One of our most experienced agents is proceeding to Belgium tonight. His mission is to contact the high personage with message from the Belgian Prime Minister, and report on suitable grounds for a Lysander pick-up.*
>
> *In accordance with our conversation this morning, he is also being instructed to examine the possibility of a sea operation, and in this connection to report to us: -*
>
> *Whether the personage could be conveyed to the Belgian coast. If so, at what point on the coast could this be done.*
>
> *Details of enemy defences at this point on the coast.*
>
> *Whether it would be possible to get hold of a boat*

> *to bring the personage out to a rendez-vous at sea, and if so at what point this could be done.*
>
> *As soon as this information reaches us, I understand Captain SLOCUM will intimate to us his further requirements.*
>
> *The actual carrying out of the operation will, in ant event, depend on Foreign Office decision as to the desirability of exfiltrating the personage, which will only be taken when we have all in readiness on the Belgian side.*
>
> *It may be relevant to mention that the personage is suffering from acute sciatica, which makes long distance travelling very difficult. It is thus probably out of the question for him to go to France where a Lysander operation would be less difficult than in Belgium.* (Ibid.)

A note in the file from the Foreign Office, addressed to Commander Johns and signed F. K. Roberts, confirmed that from the point of view of His Majesty's Government and the Belgian Government the matter was to be regarded as high priority.

> *He therefore hopes that it will be possible to proceed at once with the preliminary stage of this operation, i.e. dropping someone in Belgium to examine the position locally and report on the practical possibility of bringing Prince Charles out. At he same time, in view of the difficulties and risks in such an operation, he would wish to be consulted again when this report has been received and before any final decision is reached to lay on the actual operation.* (Ibid.)

Not mentioned in the SOE files I went through, the TV documentary, *The Children who Fought Hitler*, stated that four Dutch agents had been captured and beheaded just weeks before the team were dropped and that the Gestapo were on the look out for Wendelen.

The exact details of what happened in the month

between Elaine, Wendelen and Van de Spiegle landing in early August and the Allies' success in invading Belgium in early September 1944 are uncertain. They were said to have made their way independently to Brussels. Wendelen is said to have bribed a guard working at one of the V2 rocket sites to provide him with vital information. This was sent back to London by de Spiegle from safe houses found by Elaine in liaison with the resistance.

She also had to carry his radio set between safe houses and ensure that he was not caught transmitting by any of the 'D-Effers', a term used for the German goniometrists, the direction finders. On one occasion she was working out of town and received an urgent message from Wendelen asking her to bring the radio set back to Brussels for a transmission. As the railway system was in chaos with derailed and blown up trains and carriages blocking the lines, she had to go by road. A German officer staying at the same hotel as her, being a gentleman, insisted on his chauffeur driving them to the city in his car, even volunteering to carry her heavy suitcase. When she told him it was meat, ham and butter, he questioned whether it was for the black market. Denying it, she convinced him that it was for her family. She even gave the chauffeur a false address near Wendelen's safe house, in case the officer invited himself round later. Extremely nervous, she waved them off, desperate they wouldn't stay until she had let herself in. She had no idea whose house it was. Very luckily, the car drove off. (Elliot, S. and Fox, J. op.cit.) She reported afterwards that, "*I wasn't frightened. Maybe that's why I didn't get arrested. I didn't look frightened enough for the Germans to suspect me.*" (*The Daily Record,* 'Revealed: Amazing true stories of childhood courage during WW2', Graham Keal, 8 November 2009)

Getting Prince Charles out was a different matter. Connart told me that there had only ever been one Lysander flight to Belgium. That was on 6 December 1941 when the pilot landed in a deserted small airfield near Neufchâteau to pick up Captain Jean Cassart, an SOE agent who had been parachuted in October that year. The original choice of field at Poulseur, south of Liège had been refused as it was too close to high-tension cables.

After two months working with the LUC resistance group, its leaders were betrayed and a plane was needed urgently to get Cassart and Henri Verhaegen, his radio operator, out. There were some in the group who felt that King Léopold should have been taken back to England on the plane and Cassart was ready to let him go in his place. As it turned out, the King had not been told of the plan and the threat of being of his being deported to Germany had receded.

As the reception committee waited in the moonlight deep in the snow covered woods, they eventually heard the dull engine noise of the approaching Lysander. As soon as the lights were lit to indicate the wind direction and length of the field, the feldgendarmes arrived. Shooting broke out and, according to Freddie Clark in his *Agents by Moonlight,* the pilot, Sgt Murphy of 161 Squadron, circled the field, convinced that those to be picked up were being pursued. On seeing a dip in the field, he put on more power, overshot it, landed on the other side of the field about a quarter of a mile (400 m.) away and turned ready for take off. The two potential passengers were involved in a gun fight and very quickly he came under fire. Despite thirty bullets in the Lysander and one though his neck, Murphy managed to take off and return safely to Tempsford. Wearing a pair of his girlfriend's stockings round his neck for good luck had saved his life. Tightening them had staunched the flow of blood.

Cassart and Verhaegan, having killed several of their attackers, managed to escape but had to leave a suitcase full of reports for London behind. In them were lots of incriminating documents. Consequently, the group had to make themselves scarce. Cassart was captured in Brussels but managed to escape during his trial in Berlin and followed Verhaegen down the Comète escape line through France and out via Spain.

According to Connart, the reason for no more Lysander landings being attempted was that, with Belgium's population density being so high, there were few potential landing sites. Those who collaborated with the occupying forces and saw an approaching low-flying plane would be likely to report it. The flak was also a problem. Being more urbanised, the country bristled with heavy and light anti-aircraft guns, radar stations and night-fighter bases. It was much more concentrated than in France. Also, because Belgium was on the most direct route for RAF planes to bomb Germany, there were much greater defence networks in place. He told me that

> The vast desert plains in France were a piece of cake for Verity [Group Captain of 161 Squadron] and his mates. Much less inhabitants. France was a rather friendly country for the Germans. Resistance was almost exclusively communist until full occupation in Nov 42. De Gaulle was not yet representing anything much for the majority of the population. I'm a flight instructor and I'm always amazed when flying above France. There are landings areas almost everywhere, giant fields, and extremely scattered villages. Flying over Belgium means you only can follow railroads and major speedways. All the villages look the same and look like part of one single city. You can't land without being seen, if you are lucky enough to find a 300 yards long field without power lines and other obstacles. (Email communication with Connart, 14 July 2009)

In Thompson's memoirs about the Belgian Section, he pointed out that the long land journey to Belgium was fraught with danger. Before he was transferred, Vichy France was as dangerous as German-occupied territory. There were two heavily guarded control lines to be crossed: the 'Green Line' which passed at its northerly point through Chalons-sur-Saône, and looped round, leaving a corridor from northern France through the Spanish frontier in the southwest, and further up, the 'Red Line' which near the northern French coast, followed roughly the line of the River Somme.

Connart's research into the Belgium files showed that the SOE's plan involved sending Wendelen back, now promoted to Major. This mission involved him being parachuted into the Ardennes with the task of finding his friend 'Jean' and arranging for Prince Charles and Goffinet to move out from where they had been living clandestinely in Sart-lez-Spa, near Liège. They had to move to the chateau of Walter de Selys Longchamps at Halloy, near Ciney.

De Selys Longchamps was an important figure in Group G. Staying with him, in hiding with from the Gestapo, was 41-year-old "Monsieur Jules Bernard", an English-speaking gentleman who had been educated at Eton and Dartmouth.

There was a report, mentioned by Connart, that a young woman, who might well have been Elaine, was seen walking around the garden with Mr. Bernard, According to the west-vlaanderen website, he was known to some as 'Monsieur Richard' and, like others in the Belgian aristocracy, had helped to fund the resistance. He had a helper, Baron Robert Goffinet, the man mentioned earlier as having funded the Comète evaders.

At Sovet, not far from Ciney, was a grass runway which, as the Luftwaffe had used it during the 1940 invasion, the RAF considered it suitable for one of Tempsford's Lysander pilots to land.

On 10 August 1944, in a note stamped TOP SECRET and headed LYSANDER PICK-UP IN BELGIUM, Dobson wrote to Brigadier E. E. Mockler-Ferrymman with a copy to Air Vice Marshall A. P. Ritchie, telling them that a meeting of the Chiefs of Staff and the Foreign Secretary on 9 February had agreed that the Prince should be exfiltrated. This message had to be encoded and sent to the radio operator but, according to Connart, the radio operator was in trouble. He was hiding in a secret cave under the main road in Marloie, a few kilometres down the line from Cimey. It was owned by Louis Harsin, a worker on the railway around the edge of whose garden a long antenna had been deployed.

When one of Harsin's friends was arrested, he decided it was best to go into hiding. His house was requisitioned and two German railway workers were given lodgings there. Whether this was related to the Dutch railway workers' strike is uncertain. The German response was to bring in their own workers to manage the railway system. Maybe the two workers had been brought in to supervise this line. Under the circumstances it was impossible for the radio operator to transmit.

This was not the reason why the Prince stayed. Connart suggested that there were too many risks, the Air Ministry might have refused, the prince might have objected to going or that work on the evasion lines was in idle as many of the railways had been blown up. (Author's email communication with Philippe Connart June 8th 2009)

The last entry in the PATRON file was a note dated 23 August 1944 in which it stated that

> *There is no news so far. The agent who was sent to Belgium to lay up this operation was given instructions to consider the possibilities of an alternative to an air pick-up only if the latter was found to be impossible or if too much delay were involved.*
>
> *The present position is that we are still awaiting details in connection with the proposed ground for the pick-up and in view of the next approach of the coming moon period, it is probable that all the possibilities in this respect will be exhausted before consideration is given to the alternative method.*
> (TNA HS 6/216)

Some of the details of what actually happened were found in Wendelen's personnel file. In his report, dated

15 November 1944, he said that the day after they landed they made their way to a railway station but, unable to get to Brussels, they went to Ciney. There he contacted Walter de Selys Longchamps, "*alias Willy Gerard, who was the head of Group G in the Ardennes.*" Thanks to his help, he and Elaine were found comfortable accommodation in Brussels whilst van de Spiegle was installed in the Jemelle in the Ardennes. Elaine's debrief shed more light on her mission.

> *As the moon period was ending on August 11th, BRABANTIO tried at once to organise the Lysander operation hoping it could take place in the last days of the moon period. Therefore, he contacted JEAN DE LANDSHEERE in Brussels and arranged with BARON GOFFINET that PATRON and Major de MARRE would be transferred near the landing fields on August 11th. Meanwhile BRABANTIO had investigated the field (PHYPHY) which he found perfectly convenient once the necessary arrangements had been made for moving part of the crops. BRABANTIO tried to send through a message giving a summary description of the field. The full clock ray description necessitating at least three messages could not possibly be sent in due time for the operation to take place during that same moon period. Unfortunately, several technical hitches prevented FOXTROT from getting the messages through. BRABANTIO had to fall back on the operators working under HUGUETTE, NELLY and DELPHINE the result being that the messages reached London a long time after the end of the moon period. Meanwhile a very active search was carried out by the Police, infuriated by their inability to get hold of PATRON. They seemed to believe that PATRON was the head of the Secret Army and accordingly ordered a thorough search of the Brabant Wallon where the Secret Army was supposed to have its H.Q. and actually had it. (That search accounts for the failure of the container and*

personnel operation on VERDI at the same period.) On August 11th everybody was ready in the vicinity of the field, whose protection was to be ensured by a team of picked Group G men.

After the moon period was over, PATRON and his Ordinance Officer who had been sheltered at the Chateau D'Halloy in view of the Lysander Operation that was supposed to take place two miles away from the Chateau, went back to the PATRON's hiding place in the SPA area. BRABANTIO did several journeys to the landing field where he went as far as getting the crops removed and the field rolled, and took the clock ray description asked for by the R.A.F. The field itself was known as having been used by the Luftwaffe and consequently any movement in the neighbourhood attracted attention with the local population not to mention the Germans stationed in the nearby town of Ciney. For that reason BRABANTIO could hardly walk about pacing the field and had to be content with a clock ray description taken from the nearest cross-roads. As he was perfectly satisfied that the field was suitable for the operation, he had a shock when he eventually heard that it was not accepted by the R.A.F. whose argument seemed to be that, from the description given, two fields had been proposed, one of them being on a steep slope and the other one being much too small. BRABANTIO is very sorry that the R.A.F. would not show more confidence in his repeated statements to the effect that the field was suitable. Nevertheless, he was, and he still is, prepared to take a 10 to 1 bet with any R.A.F. Officer that a medium sized bomber can be landed safely on that field in day-time and that any average pilot would find it easy to land a Lysander on it by night if only the operation were attempted.

About 20th August PATRON let us know that owing to the military situation he wondered whether *the pick up operation was still advisable and we decided to put forward the question to London. Before we got the answer things had moved so quickly that PATRON had decided to remain in hiding waiting for the arrival of the Allied forces. Before the events had led him to take that decision, he had been very keen on the operation and was quite willing to run the risks involved. BRABANTIO feels quite confident that the operation had every chance to be successful as far as the landing of the aircraft, his protection while landing and his take off were concerned.* (TNA HS 6/44)

The real reason, according to Johns, was that, when the moment came, Prince Charles was suffering acutely from some rheumatic or arthritic complaint and could not face a long journey in the cramped conditions in the back of a Lysander. As liberation was imminent, the operation was scrubbed. (Johns, op.cit. p.170)

Elaine's personnel file in the Ondersectie Notariaat Archieven at MoD Belgium in Brussels, contains a letter that she wrote to the Minister of Defence in which she said that she was "*behind the lines, mission BRABANTIO, during the periods 4th August 1944 to 3rd September,*" (TNA HS6/112) a few days before the liberation of Brussels. In an interview after the war, she told how, when the first British soldiers drove into Brussels on 5 September, she sent a request to London asking for her uniform to be dropped so that she could be seen with her 'wings', the badge she won for completing her parachute jump training at Ringway. Local people could hardly believe it.

The people who saw me in uniform, with my wings on, they kind of looked at me and said: 'Are you English? You're a parachutist? ' and I said, 'Yes.' But I was the only, you know, British girl in uniform, apart from the German girls. It was an uproar. I couldn't even walk. They were carrying me on their shoulders to show off. Look at the parachutist. These were some of the happiest days in my life. Everyone seemed to be so proud of me and to kiss me and to love me and there was such a lot of hugging and drinking and eating and invitations from people I'd never seen before in my life. It was a fabulous feeling. (Ibid.)

In her debrief, she said that she only once had any trouble when she had to shake off someone who was following her. She found the work much easier than she had anticipated and all the people she tried to contact were most helpful. The only regret she had was not having arrived sooner and being able to work more. In Wendelen's report during his debrief he told his interrogator that she had

...showed a great devotion to duty and complete disregard for danger. She very efficiently organised the W/Ts protection under the guidance of BRABANTIO. She fulfilled most satisfactorily every task of courier or others with which she had been trusted. There is no doubt that she would have been trusted with more responsibilities if the liberation had not so sadly interfered with the BRABANTIO mission (although of course nobody minded really). (Ibid.)

After the war, Elaine told an interviewer from 'Histoires', a documentary programme on *Canvas*, one of Belgium's two public TV channels:

My chef de mission said that I was to come to Ciney (southeast of Namur) *and look after this important gentleman. I met him [there], I thought he was very charming. We used to talk, play ping-pong together, we used to go walking in the woods. And once we were away from other people, he would speak to me in English. His English was fluent and we had a lot of fun. [...] He used to question me*

> *about London, and London during the wartime, and what was happening. [...] I thought he was somebody in the resistance who was very important. So, I was his liaison between London and here, I used to code and decode messages. And we were trying to find a small landing ground so the Lysander could come and fetch him. Because the idea was that we wanted to get him to England.*
>
> *... When eventually we did find a landing ground, [Sovet] ... it was already so late in the war. The Allies were arriving so quickly after Normandy, that he decided he didn't want to leave because it was too late. That he wouldn't have time to get out of the plane in London, before getting into another plane back to Belgium. So the mission was dropped.* (Histories, Canvas TV)

When Prince Charles was appointed Prince Regent in 1945, he gave Elaine an award and she claims that it was only at the ceremony that she realised that he was the Prince of Flanders. Her file in the Ondersectie Notariaat Archieven says that,

> *Lieutenant MADDEN accepted spontaneously a special mission. Despite the dangers, she agreed and acquitted herself showing understanding and leadership in the services that were requested. She demonstrated the highest patriotic qualities.* (HRG-A/N-Archives 2363363 Madden)

Further detail appeared in her debrief to the SOE with her admitting that,

> *There was no time to work on my personal mission owing to the fact that I was "Courrier" for Odette. The majority of the time I didn't know which mission I was working for, but information could be obtained from Odette's report. I travelled considerably in the Ardennes, carrying messages, transmitting sets and bringing the revolvers back to*

Brussels. I was put in contact with Huguette and did some "courier" for him. Apart from that, I was in charge of the "service de protection" for Foxtrot and recruited three people to help us. Two were permanent staff and third part-time. I was part of the "service de protection" on every occasion and usually transported the soul myself to the house elected. The finding of safe houses was also left to me. I never had any trouble of any kind, except once when I was followed for several hours by a suspicious looking character. I managed to shake him off by taking various trams and wandering around the town. This happened after I had been to rendezvous with C. Lapoivre (operational name unknown).

Help and assistance were given by Mlle Denise Leplat, 19 rue de Anges, Liège and Jean Smets (address unknown) who worked full-time as "service de protection". Also Anton Smets who worked part-time. The two sisters Lucy and Jeanne Rouffignon, rue Chants d'Oiseaux, Bruxelles, also helped considerably by letting us transmit from their house and in helping me find other houses to transmit from. (TNA HS 6/112)

Denise Leplat

After Elaine's typed up debrief notes, there were three pages of additional information in her file, notes following an interview that the SOE had with Denise Leplat, the young Belgian girl mentioned above. She was interrogated on 23 February 1945 by Captain Watt. Whether the interview took place in Belgium or in England is unknown. Why she was interviewed will become clear later.

Denise's father, a doctor in Liège, had been the contact given to André Wendelen when he was parachuted into the outskirts of the city on 27 January 1942. A lieutenant in SOE, Wendelen had numerous codenames including *Limbosch*, and *Archangel*. *Tybalt*, *Hector* and *Brabantio* were the names of his missions. He was the organiser of one of twenty-five resistance groups in Belgium, work for which he was subsequently awarded the Military Cross.

Jean Brillant, the radio operator who landed with him, was provided with accommodation at Doctor Leplat's house where he got to know Denise. Although she was only seventeen and a half at the time, she was keen to do some active work for the resistance. Wendelen gave her the job of being his courier between Liège and Brussels.

Every Monday morning, on the pretence that she was visiting her grandmother, Denise would catch the train and hide the messages she had to deliver in her magazine or in her shopping basket. She claimed during the interview that she did not know whether the messages were in code or '*en clair*'.

When she first started clandestine work in 1942, German controls were lax but they intensified over the next few years. A *feldgendarme* and a plain clothes civilian often questioned people on trams or at street corners but, as was found in many occupied countries, women were rarely thoroughly searched and only a superficial search of parcels and shopping baskets was carried out. The worst place, she said, was Louvain, where everything that was thought might contain arms was searched. On one occasion her valise was gone through but, luckily, nothing incriminating was found.

In January 1944, following her brother's escape to England, she took over as courier for Group G. Her brother had been provided papers by Hector (André) and spent three months travelling along the Comète escape line through Paris and Rouen, eventually crossing into Spain. Stepping into his shoes, Denise carried out missions for Freddy Schenus, another resistance leader, and used "*boîtes aux letters*" between Wendelen and his adjutants, George Marchand, an engineer in the steel industry and another man, Victor Carbonelle.

When Denise was not couriering, she occasionally got involved with preparing explosives for sabotage tasks and, according to the notes,

> … *transport them to the chef of the team which was to carry out the operation. It was customary for Freddy to telephone her the day before the operation, or contact her in some other way, and make a rendezvous for six that night to prepare the charges. When this work was completed informant would carry the charges in a sack either concealed in a basket or merely in the front of her bicycle. Frequently she did not know to whom she had to make the delivery, and in this case pass words were used. Informant received her instruction for preparing the charges from Wendelen. This sabotage work was for the Partisans, but although informant was most anxious to do more sabotage work she was not permitted to, and only assisted in one operation. The explosives they used were of a very inferior quality, but some very good plastic was parachuted from England. The charges for pylons were usually angle charges, but when they had run out of Plastic, T.N.T. in the commercial form had to be used. This was difficult to handle so the charges were made up in empty tins with a detonator in the middle. The whole was then attached to the pylon by means of wire, usually about three or four*

charges per pylon were used, each charge containing about 900 grams of explosive. The sabotage teams varied in size from three to six men, but informant knew little of the organisation. (TNA HS 6/112)

When Denise suggested to some of her friends that they might like to do some clandestine work, most had been unwilling. She suggested to her interviewer that they might already have been involved and did not want to work for another resistance unit. She herself was approached on several occasions with a view to do resistance work, but she adopted a disinterested attitude, saying that the work was too dangerous.

The only sabotage operation Denise took part in was with Wendelen. After preparing some explosives in a hotel room in Liège, they went to the railway line where she acted as a lookout whilst he set the charge.

They were both armed with revolvers. The charges were 1½ sticks of plastic in two charges one metre apart, connected with Cortex [explosive cord]. The method of initiating the charge was a detonator on the end of Bickford [fuse], and they used enough Bickford to enable them to get a short distance away before the explosion occurred. The operation was carried out in the late evening, and they had time to get to the nearby village before the explosion, and walked along innocently as if they were lovers. Nobody suspected them, and the operation was successful. (Ibid)

What was described by Johns as the most successful sabotage operation, what became known as *La Grande Coupure,* took place on 15 January 1944, between 2000 hours and 2300 hours. About twenty inadequately guarded pylons in isolated parts of Belgium were blown up. A further eight were put out of action the following day.

> The entire industrial area of the Borinage was trapped without power. The industrial areas of Liège, Mechelen, Dendermonde and surrounding cities had no power. The effects ranged further. The German Rhineland suffered from the effects of this sabotage because the Group G had also dynamited the lines into Germany so that not only was Belgian industry without power, but also the Ruhr basin, the heart of German industry and the industrial areas of northern France. (Ibid)

The repair of the distribution system required enormous manpower and estimates of between ten and fifteen million man-hours of work were lost when industrial production came to a standstill. The sabotage brought home to the German command that the Belgian resistance was led and organised to the extent that it could carry out similar attacks in the future. (Johns, op.cit.p.163)

Jean, Wendelen's radio operator, made eighteen transmissions from a room on the second floor of Denise's father's house. As the Germans had banned wireless sets, anyone found transmitting would therefore have to be a spy.

Denise acted as a lookout, tapping the central heating pipe that ran up through the ceiling into the room where Jean was working. On hearing it, he would hide the set under the floorboards and rush downstairs and do some washing up. His cover was that the doctor employed him as a domestic servant.

After an unsuccessful search of the premises, the only safe house Denise could find where the occupants were willing to let Jean stay was very close by. It was lived in by two ladies who had worked for the resistance during the 1914-18 war. It could have been the one referred to earlier on rue du Chant d'Oiseau, owned by the two sisters, Lucy and Jeanne Rouffignon. No sooner than he moved in, he restarted transmitting and the direction-finding restarted.

> Informant noticed a Citroen with an aerial coming down the street and immediately gave the danger signal. These cars would make detours around a certain block, and men with a listening apparatus in their ear were also used. As soon as the informant gave the danger signal

Jean cut the transmission and they all scattered. Informant left in a lorry for Liège, and she later learned that Jean was surprised by the Germans the next day during his transmission and arrested.
(Ibid)

The two ladies were arrested with him, and, at the time of Denise's interview, were reported as being in prison in Germany. The day following Jean's arrest, she realised that her father's surgery was being watched by an agent provocateur. The file has several words about him blacked out, possibly his name, but stated that he was a young man of medium height, fairly good looking, brown hair, no distinguishing marks but short-sighted. He had joined the waiting list in the surgery but started asking Denise why she visited Brussels so often and what she did there.

Worried that she had been denounced to the Gestapo, she went to stay in the countryside with her cousin, Michèle Pèriot. She had to lie low for six weeks until she was provided with a back-dated employment certificate. Although her cousin worked in the Sûreté, the Belgian police, he also participated in a reception committee, collecting canisters dropped by parachute from planes flown from RAF Tempsford and Harrington.

When her cousin was arrested in February 1944, she stayed with an uncle. Many members of the *Mouvement Nationaliste Belge*, one of the resistance groups, were arrested following denunciations to the Gestapo. According to her interview notes, one was caught and before any message could be got through to warn the others, they were arrested at the rendezvous. This forced Denise to go into hiding until May 1945 when Belgium was finally liberated.

Although the Belgian resistance played a large part in their country's liberation, exactly how important Elaine's role was can only be surmised. After all the celebrations, she was recalled to London and briefed for another mission. It was to return to Belgium and accompany a group of liberating forces visiting the German concentration camps in an attempt to find missing SOE agents. What she found was horrifying and distressing. Only two Belgian agents had survived. She was later awarded the Croix de Guerre and 'Mentioned in Dispatches' for her bravery.

The anonymous Belgian blonde

In Johns' wartime memoirs, 'Within Two Cloaks' he provides details of the staff he worked with in the Belgian Section and some of the agents he sent in. There was no mention of Elaine, Olga or Frédérique but he stated that:

Another name I have forgotten (and would not mention even if I remembered) was that of a young and exceptionally attractive Belgian girl, with long blonde hair, a beautiful slim figure, intensely blue eyes, and last but not least highly intelligent. Her husband or fiancé had been arrested by the Gestapo, taken to Germany where he was tortured in one of the notorious concentration camps and then hanged as a spy. The girl herself had escaped to England and volunteered to join SOE for eventual parachuting into her country, her personal objective being to revenge her husband or fiancé's execution. After the usual training period, she was dropped into Belgium on a mission to proceed independently into Brussels, and then patronise the bars and hotels most frequented by German officers. She was to associate with the latter, offering her services in bed if necessary, and then arrange for these Germans to be beaten up and put out of action for a long time by one of the Resistance groups' assassination squads. Some of her victims were liquidated by meeting with 'fatal accidents'. Apart from her successes in the field, she was also able from time to time to relay to us important military intelligence resulting from the 'pillow indiscretions' of her clients. (Johns, P. *Within Two Cloaks*, William Kimber, (1979), p.161)

Who she was, whether she underwent SOE training and when she was infiltrated have not yet come to light. However, there are elements in her story that are similar to that of the next woman sent in.

Olga Jackson

Searching for information on Olga Jackson, the woman parachuted in the same night as Elaine, I found an intriguing reference on the Adam Matthew Publications website's list of all the SOE missions. Thirty-eight of the agents sent into Belgium were given female field names. Whether this was meant to confuse the enemy remains unknown. The one I was looking for read:

> *EMELIA. Belgium, August 1944, Mrs Olga Jackson, field name Babette, independent propaganda mission for undermining of morale in Brussels, Ghent, Liege, Antwerp, Charleroi; organisation of prostitution circuit aimed at German officers.* (http://www.adam-matthew-publications.co.uk/digital_guides/ special_operations_executive_series_1_parts_1_t o_5/SOE-Summary-of-Operations-in-Western-Europe.aspx)

An enquiry into Olga's personnel file in the National Archives revealed a fascinating story, worth detailing as it shows what other kinds of intrigues were thought up by the Political Warfare Executive (PWE).

On the night of 4 August, the same day Elaine was dropped, 34-year-old Olga was also parachuted into farmland outside Brussels. Whether they had known each other before the war, met in London, trained together at Winterfold and Arisaig, got their parachute wings at Ringway and attended the 'Finishing School' at Beaulieu remains unknown. It is possible they were flown out in the same plane.

Correspondence with Philippe Connart of belgiumww2 website revealed that she was born on 6 January 1909, was called Olga Thioux and was a British citizen. Her personnel file mentions nothing of her early life. Foot stated that she was born in Belgium but 'married an English husband [retired Royal Artillery major] and had lived in England since 1935. She had a strong, self-confident, humorous personality, and was a junior FANY officer. She joined SOE in March 1944.' (Foot. op.cit.p.377) According to Lee Richards, the psychological warfare historian, she had been Belgian's first female professional parachutist. (Richards, Lee, *Black Art: British Clandestine Psychological Warfare against the Third Reich*, www.pyswar.org, 2010, p.36)

For whatever reason, she jumped before her luggage and two companions, 'Eugénie' and 'Yvonne'. Their intended drop zone was supposed to be just under eight miles (13.5 km) north of Hals, near Ledeberg. Instead, she landed just under two miles (3 km) from Pamel, a small village between Ninove and Brussels and was not able to make contact with the other two agents, Given the demise of the agents sent in earlier, she was dropped blind, with no reception committee waiting to welcome her.

Whether 'Eugénie' and 'Yvonne' really were women and what their real names were proved to be a mystery. The only additional mention of them in Olga's file was their mission names, *MENAS* and *CIMBER*. Checking these names on the above website showed that Eugénie's *MENAS* mission was to contact Samoyède II, Samoyède I was Frédéric Veldekens's propaganda mission for pre- and post-liberation work and jamming German wireless installations with the aim of helping Allies from D-Day in the use of the press, cinema and radio. Foot identified Samoyède II as Frans Marten, whose job was to ensuring the continuation of Freddy's work. The *CIMBER* mission involved the transmission of microfiche messages.

Connart shed light on their missions. *MENAS* was Léon Chabart, alias *Carlier* and *Eugénie* and the *MENAS* mission was also referred to as *STENTOR*. *CIMBER* stands for Civil Mission for Belgian Relief. Etienne Plissart, alias *Yvonne, Perichon* and *Jean-Pierre Petit,* was a lawyer who had to organise the August wheat harvest so that it would not fall into

German hands, avoiding a post-liberation famine on Belgian soil (like in Holland where the Germans had time to remove all the Dutch food stores).

According to Olga's file, after hiding her parachute in some bushes, she made her way to Brussels, but minus her luggage. It had come down elsewhere. With the help of someone she met on the road who was convinced she was a black marketeer, she avoided the checkpoint and at 0700 arrived at her safe house, the home of Madame and Monsieur René de Pot, the Police Brigadier.

On showing him her identity papers, he was suspicious but a personal message following the BBC news convinced him of her credentials. With the help of one of his friends, he got her better identity cards but, as this friend was arrested the following day, she had to be quickly provided with others, just in case he talked. Arrangements were made for her to meet M. Schakewitz, the Joint Police Commissioner and Chief Inspector of Police, Although he listened with interest to her plans, he did not show much enthusiasm for her enterprise. However, he did promise to help. There was no mention of her being reunited with her luggage or companions.

She then went to Liège and met Frans Banneux. Whether he was another police official, government or resistance member was not made clear except that she made arrangements with him for her safe house in case the Germans found out what she was up to. What else she did whilst in Liège was not mentioned.

Foot considered it an 'odd mission' as she was unable to speak a word of German, yet had to introduce herself to as many German senior staff as she could. (Foot, op.cit.p.377)

When she returned to Brussels three days later, she had another meeting with the Chief Inspector and insisted she be introduced to Monsieur Delecourt, the King's Public Prosecutor. Whilst she was waiting, he introduced her to Monsieur de Lobel, the Chief Bailiff, who agreed to help her. He provided her with a room in

M. Jungelaus' Brussels office and allocated two women to assist her in collecting information on the private and public lives of important German figures stationed in Belgium. Over time they compiled a list, which included:

> "*General von Falkenhausen Alexander, Dr. Reeder President Eggert, von Harbou Obest. Von Schon, von Graushaar General, Dr Bayer, Bennewitz Hauptbannfuhrer, von Hammerstein Freiherr Lieutenant-General, Dr. Schulze Adolf, Landesgruppenleiter, Dr. Gentzke, von Clear General, Dr. Busch, Gayler, Angelmann Lieutenant-Colonel, Bruns Major General, von Werder, Dr. Mallia, Schmidt, Dr. Griesbauer, Feldberg, Schindlmayer and Moskopf*". (TNA HS 6/84)

The 'independent propaganda' she was involved with was "*to complement the campaign already being waged by the Mandrill organisation*". An Internet search revealed that this was a Political Intelligence Department mission sent into Belgium in 1943 to liaise with the existing *CORDIER* mission to demoralise support for the Germans and co-ordinate the reception of propaganda in Lille, Liège and Ghent.

In Lee Richard's *Black Art*, he referred to the 'Porcupine'/'Mandrill' mission as

> ...perhaps the largest black propaganda distribution network created in Belgium. Its general objective was to demoralise German soldiers stationed in Belgium. More specifically it was to:
> Create two or three Reception Committees in order to receive material despatched from England;
> Distribute propaganda material amongst German troops in Belgium;
> Make clear to the Belgian population, by means of the clandestine press, the role which they could play in the work of demoralisation of German soldiers;

Develop writing on hoardings and monuments, and disseminate stickers, tracts and pamphlets and also diffuse rumours;
Sabotage Field Post Offices and mail destined for German soldiers and assist German military deserters;
And finally, set up printing presses for the printing of propaganda material on the spot. (TNA HS 6/142, Porcupine – Mandrill mission report, 5 October 1943; Richards, op.cit. p.34)

'Porcupine', Richards identified as 36-year-old Jean Coyette, the leader of the mission whose main responsibilities were to make contact with Belgian resistance fighters and organise networks for the dissemination of black propaganda. Once this was completed, he appointed Ernest Piot, the former General Secretary of the Belgian Labour Party, to succeed him and returned to England via Switzerland. 'Mandrill', the mission's sub-organiser was Henri Filot, and both men had been parachuted into Belgium on 13 April 1943, three months before Olga.

The mission's first supply drop was organised for the night of 11/12 August in the region of Aywaille. Two containers were dropped. The first was full of black propaganda material and the second contained weapons and food. The supplies were initially transported to Liege and stowed away in the basement of a university building. From there the propaganda was sent to Brussels and handed out to a number of regional distribution networks. Various means were employed to deliver the propaganda into the hands of German soldiers. The Brussels network had the names and addresses of all German officers and soldiers billeted in private houses in the city. Envelopes of propaganda were sent directly through the post to those on the list. Elsewhere workmen and tradesmen with access to barracks helped with the dissemination. At one barracks in Namur several German officers were accused of spreading the propaganda and subsequently arrested. In theatres and cinemas regularly frequented by Germans, charwomen and cleaners deposited propaganda on the seats and Belgian staff working in restaurants and soldiers' canteens placed items on tables or in the lavatories. One enterprising female distributor gained access to a German troop train waiting at a railway station platform. Before the soldiers embarked, she managed to place propaganda in each of the train's compartments. Utilising these methods most of the material received in August was circulated in the towns of Antwerp, Brussels, Charleroi, Liege, Louvain and Namur. (Richards, op.cit. p.35; TNA FO 898/94, PWE Missions in Belgium: Agents, activities, reports, messages and correspondence. TNA HS 6/142, Report on interview with Mandrill, 26 January 1944)

Olga's work, her mission papers stressed, was

"*in no way connected with espionage and it must be clearly understood that your task is not the collection of military information. By doing so you would be liable not only to jeopardise your own security but also the success of the mission itself*". (TNA HS 6/84)

It included finding every opportunity to tell people of the imminent arrival of the Allies, their impending liberation and release from the yolk of German oppression. Members of the Belgian Resistance had to be told to wait until they were given instructions by the Allies' High Command to take action. She had to recruit and instruct responsible people to help with her work of disseminating rumours and lies about the enemy and about an imminent Allied landing. This included setting up a radio listening centre, typing false stories to be leaked to the media and narrating them to people she met. Her list of people to meet included those dealing with news broadcasts, editors, radio announcers, technicians and Morse operators. She had instructions as to what action the civilian population had to take following the Allies' arrival, in particular the technicians in the gas, electricity, water, rubbish, railway, tramway and telecommunication industries as well as factory workers, road workers, dock workers, mechanics and miners.

She had to disseminate supposedly Belgian police-generated information about the Allies' plans, their estimated troop numbers, predictions of their movements, military equipment, weapons and food stocks. Although not mentioned, one guesses it was exaggerated or lies. Where possible, she, and those supporting her, had to cause delays and obstruct collaboration with the Germans. She had to undermine their and their collaborators' positions by spreading malicious rumours about conflicts between them, denunciations and recriminations and what those on the side of the Allies might do to them.

Detailed notes had to be made of the preparations the Germans were making for the invasion, what demolition work they were undertaking and what their troop movements were so as to supply it to the Allies when they arrived. Attempts had to be made to warn the Allies as to the Germans' eventual retreat and to try to ensure that their supplies were spread over a wide area.

Another task was to undermine the morale of the German troops, to depress them and make them nervous by spreading stories that parts of Germany were being overrun by Allied troops, that German villages were being bombed and how other German soldiers stationed in Belgium were becoming irritated and exasperated by what they saw as indiscipline.

According to Olga's instructions, she had to find an organiser in Brussels, Liége, Anvers, Ghent, Namur and Charleroi and provide them with a list of generally high-ranking German military or administrative officials to 'attack'.

It will be necessary to establish the identity of the Belgian and other non-German mistresses kept by German officers and officials and then to determine how many of them can be utilised either because they are good patriots or for other reasons. Those selected should, through suitable outlets, be approached. Tactics at this point will depend entirely upon the type of individual concerned but in order to obtain their co-operation it will not be necessary to use financial or other material inducements. The women thus to be approached will fall roughly into two categories:

(i) Those who have a genuine personal affection for their German masters,

(ii) Those who from force of circumstances or otherwise find it easier thus to earn their living and whose personal feelings are not to any extent involved.

As regards (i) these may be the most difficult to enlist but having once convinced them good results should be obtained. It may not be necessary to take this category into your confidence provided they are convinced that defeat for Germany means added danger for their protector unless he covers himself. The line to be taken is that they will clearly wish to do the best for their "friends". Whether or not an appeal should be made to their patriotism must be left to the consideration of the person contacting them. The "amie" must first be thoroughly convinced that Germany has lost the war and her thoughts must be directed to what is to become of her "friend". This thought she must discreetly sow in the mind of the officer or official himself, thus inducing him to defer a decision for a few weeks or months? And if he is not killed on one of the fronts what will he find when he gets home, after most of the others? Or will he, realising how things are going, take steps to see that he at least gets back to Germany alive. What is happening to his family with all the foreign workers at home? Who is to protect them if there is an armed uprising in Germany. How is he viewed by his men and the Belgians? Will the latter give him a good character or is he a "war criminal"? Other German officers are already taking steps for their own protection and the higher the rank the more active has been the urge to anticipate the future.

The subject must be introduced discreetly and not exaggerated and progress judged in the light of the "protector's" reactions. If it is clear that he has already been thinking along such lines himself, progress can be more rapid. If however, it is patent that the subject cannot be seduced from his duty by such means then he should be induced to exaggerate any weaknesses he may possess, drinking, general self-indulgence, laziness, gambling.

With younger officers, particularly if they are of an adventurous type, it will be necessary to adopt different tactics.

They should be shown that their authority is nearly over and the "good times" that went with it. They should be encouraged in any vices they may have and led to excesses in self-indulgence. They should similarly be encouraged to neglect their duties and finally if so inclined to desert altogether to some occupation in which there is a future.

It may be desirable to offer financial assistance to this class of woman, though it should not be on a lavish scale. (Ibid)

Ideally, Olga had to recruit loyal and dependable proprietors or tenants of these brothels who would pass on instructions to the women employed there. No attempt was to be made to contact German-run brothels, though non-German women employed there may be approached. They had not got to provoke or give their clients any grounds for reprisals but had to make seemingly innocent questions and remarks. Amongst those suggested were to emphasise with regret the level of Germany's moral and political decline, the decadence and ruin that was menacing it and the dark future facing the country if the war continued.

They had to underline the regret that Germany was committing treason by allying the white race alongside the 'Yellow Peril' - the Japanese. During British and American bombing raids, they had to show intense fear and express awe at what potential they had. They were encouraged to spread stories about the enormous damage that was being done by the bombing in Germany, ask whether a miracle was possible that would stop the progressive destruction of the entire country and enquire how many years they would have to endure. They had to sympathetically ask about how their wives and families were, whether they had been evacuated or requisitioned for compulsory labour.

In Ian Dear's *Sabotage and Subversion: Stories from the Files of the SOE and OSS,* he detailed a two-page pornographic leaflet Olga may well have distributed. Sefton Delmer, the Director of Special Operations to Enemy and Satellite countries for Britain's secret propaganda department, the Political Warfare Executive, came up with a plan of demoralising German troops. It was meant to make them worry about what might be happening to their wives, girlfriends and sisters when there were millions of male foreign workers in Germany. Under the heading *Lieb Vaterland magst ruhig sein* (Dear Fatherland you may rest assured), was a very gloomy picture of a snow-covered soldier's grave somewhere on the Eastern Front. The heading was the first line of a very famous German patriotic song from the days of the Kaiser 'The Watch of the Rhine'. Overleaf was another caption and picture but, instead of the caption being the second line of the song, *Fest steht und true die Wacht am Rhein* (Firm stands and true the watch on the Rhine), it read *Fest steckt's und true der Fremdarbeiter 'rein*

(Firmly sticks it and true, the foreign worker in), and underneath it was a coloured picture of a naked girl, painted in the photographic style so favoured by Hitler, who is about to lower herself onto the erect penis of some dark-haired, dark-skinned non-German. How effective they were Delmer did not know but he claimed they improved the morale of those who distributed them. (Dear, I. *Sabotage and Subversion: Stories from the Files of the SOE and OSS,* Arms and Armour, (1998), p.136)

They had to show fear about epidemics, venereal disease and other ailments which were ravaging the country, frequently ask for explanations and whether it was true that a typhoid epidemic had broken out in a distant region. They had to spread the story of a new flu epidemic coming from the East and remind the Germans of the Spanish flu epidemic that followed the Great War which killed about eighteen million people. They had to express doubt whether there was sufficient medicine, clothes and food.

It was suggested they spread around the slogan "Schluss" (The End) and ask what the significance of the griffon was on all the walls and in the toilets. They were to reinforce the natural feeling of envy about the high number of government members and top officials who had left the country and were living in comfort, in safety after having enriched themselves. They had to emphasise the laziness caused by five years of war, ten years of mobilisation, the long hours of work and the difficult living conditions. They had to accentuate the bad feeling there was about fewer imports and the voluntary reductions people were expected to accept. They had to deplore the inevitable hypocrisy caused by such grievances, especially when many of those who were suffering could see important Germans living a good life.

To incite or assist a German officer to desert requires very careful planning and the seed must be planted very carefully and nourished without apparent intention. However, when an officer has demonstrated his considered intention to desert, help should be given him. He will require two essentials, first civilian clothes and second a temporary hide out. Suitable addresses should be given to him and in both cases he should be required to pay for them. (Ibid)

One has to presume that Olga was involved in such arrangements as well as arranging the writing and sending of anonymous letters to officers' wives. These, she was recommended, had to be written on the type of paper that could then be obtained at any stationers, to have no address on them and be posted from one of the central post offices. Her advice was that they

...should not normally be written in a threatening vein but rather in the guise of a well-wisher or friend warning her of the misfortune which will befall her or the treatment planned for Germans and their wives. Reference should also be made to the risks run by her husband, of the necessity of his securing employment after the German army had been defeated. (Ibid)

There was also advice on how she could use vice to target those already known to have "*vicious habits, those susceptible to acquire them or those suffering from diseases rendering them particularly susceptible to demoralisation*". The aim was to lower their efficiency and encourage them to neglect their duties. The information in the section on drugs mentioned that drug traffickers had been arrested in Brussels who were selling opium with a street value at 60,000 francs a kilo. To put this in perspective, Olga was provided with 15,000 francs a month for spending, 10,000 for accommodation, 15,000 for clothes and 3,500 for postage. The opium had been grown in countries like Burma, which had developed its black market economy by increasing their production of oil from poppies. It would only be possible for Olga or her contacts to find out who the drug users were through loyal officers but that they would only be able to get hold of drugs through theft from military pharmacies or drug dealers. It was extremely difficult to get hold of products such as cocaine, heroin and morphine because they had almost disappeared from the market place. They had to avoid offering such "merchandise" to serious Germans because they would almost certainly inform their superiors who would make enquiries as to where they had come from. Importantly, they had not to let them fall into the hands of the Belgians.

The only places where the drugs should be on sale were to be in night clubs or other places specialising in such trade, like opium dens. Some individuals, such as pimps, could be supplied with them, as long as they would be able to resell them and make a reasonable profit. However, if they were offered to the wrong people, they would immediately believe it was "*a truly shocking and dangerous business*".

> *Doctors, Private V.D. Specialists and Clinics*
> *The co-operation of those of the above known to be patronised by German officers and officials, should be sought. The patient who suffers or believes himself to suffer from V.D. is particularly liable to be demoralised and the object here is to induce doctors to play up to this weakness to the ultimate demoralisation of the subject. Some difficulty may be anticipated as the more serious members of the medical profession are unlikely on moral grounds to co-operate but on the other hand this field covers a number of quacks and near-quacks to whom the same considerations would not supply.* (Ibid)

Officers, she was told, had a great pleasure in drinking alcohol and often broke the rules and paid a lot of money to get hold of it. Drinking spirits that had been fortified was on the increase but there were cases of adulterated and dangerous spirits. To further the Allies' aims she was encouraged to get hold of spirits of doubtful origin. If they could only be supplied to the Germans it would be perfect but it was acknowledged that unfortunately, it would not be the case.

With regards to jealousy, Olga and her contacts, were to consider two forms, those targeting the German wives or girlfriends and those who had 'field mattresses', Belgian girlfriends. The first group had to be told that the massive increase in foreign workers in Germany was creating a special situation. She would be provided with pamphlets and leaflets and be given suggested graffiti, conversations and rumours to spread amongst the German soldiers. There were not very many men left in Germany and those who were, were too old, too young, wounded, or infirm and had their own wives. It had been a long time for their wives, sisters and daughters to have been left alone, especially now that there were formidable numbers of foreign men working in Germany, men who had been sent because they were fit and healthy, the very great majority of whom "*sont originaires de races aux facultés beaucoup plus amoureuses que celle des Allemands (Italians, Français, Belges, etc)*". The nervousness of the Allied bombing and their privations must "*relâcher les consciences*".

CINEMAS, THEATRES, ETC.

It is anticipated that however willing the managers and proprietors of such establishments may be to co-operate the limit within which they will be able to will be very narrow.

Cinema managers will have very little scope in their choice of films, but where they are able to do so they should present those stressing the pleasures of peace and the horror of bombing (civilian populations, enemy); films implying the ultimate liberation of the occupied countries and the return to normal occupation of the inhabitants.

As regard theatres the situation is more difficult. Where possible plays, operas, etc, in which liberation or democratic themes appear should be presented. Tunes, songs, etc, which are identified with similar sentiments should be chosen.

Last war songs, Tipperary, Pack up your Troubles, Over There (?) Décor should be so displayed as fortuitously to represent the Allied and national colours – without risk of reprisals – reminding the enemy of approaching defeat. (Ibid)

There were instructions on different types of rumours to be spread amongst the Germans and the list of those who might help included drug traffickers and fraudsters, railway employees, waiters in cafes, hairdressers, priests, doctors, members of the resistance, sales representatives, gossips, people in queues and a group described as "Les filles de vie".

The fact is that this kind of woman is frequently in contact with Germans. That they often speak of what's going on in the war is doubtful as it wouldn't be commercial. Moreover, night clubs etc, are frequently under German police surveillance. It's inevitable that with women, and particularly with these kinds of women – many soldiers let themselves go and confide in them. They think of them a bit like comforters. Although many of these women are very patriotic, it is only with great difficulty possible to envisage them being of use. And yet, if a rumour is convincingly presented it will be passed from one Belgian or another who visits these places before the beginning of the evening. In offering a glass (not two, or there'll be financial interest and risks of exaggerated dependency), he will be able to appear the "Man in the know" and secretly to take these women into his confidence. (Ibid)

There was plenty of money to finance the EMELIA mission. Before leaving England, Olga had been supplied with 248,500 Belgian francs in 100 franc notes, presumably in a money belt. Two 1,000 French franc notes, 100 Spanish peseta notes and 4,075 US dollars in mixed notes were hidden in a box of talc to be used on her way back to England three months later. A letter, photograph and two coins, probably gold, were hidden in her nail brush. There were also details of passwords and replies for her rendezvous, including those needed in Spain and Portugal.

Her file refers to her throughout as *Jenicot* but she had several other cover names. As she had no radio operator, she had to sign letters to SOE post boxes in Barcelona and Lisbon as *Zoe*. When she planned her escape through Spain she was to be known as *Irene Thompson*.

In Foot's *"SOE in the Low Countries"* he referred to Mrs Jackson but made no mention of alcohol, drugs or prostitution. He thought it was

> *an odd mission: though she spoke not a word of German, her task was to introduce herself to as many senior German staff officers as she could, and proceed to rot their morale by explaining to them that Germany had already lost the war. In the few weeks that turned out to be available to her, she set about her task with such considerable aplomb that she was mentioned in dispatches for courage and enterprise; concrete results were necessarily slight.* (Foot, op.cit. p.377)

How successful was mission EMELIA? There was nothing in her personnel file that gives any indication. Maybe the fact that the Allies were able to force the Germans back into Germany after only a few weeks is a measure of how her propaganda might have demoralised some of their officers and troops.

Madeleine Fouconnier

In Hugh Verity's autobiography, *We Landed by Moonlight*, he mentions flying a Lysander on 17/18 October 1943 to a field just over a mile (2 km) north-north-east of Vandrimare, east-south-east of Rouen to pick up

Georges Coeckelbergh, a Belgian radio operator and Madeleine Fauconnier. Operation ENTRACTE was his third attempt to drop Deweer, a Belgian radio operator, codenamed *Speed*. He specified that it was an operation for Delbo-Phénix, whose agents were being looked after in Hotel de la Poste by Mme Jaffré. Her husband had already been arrested and the Gestapo were closing in. Madeleine was a Belgian spy, codenamed *'Claire'*, who later became Madame Lovinfosse. Whether she had married George de Lovinfosse, a Belgian businessman, is uncertain. He had helped the British Expeditionary Forces in 1940 and escaped to England. In June 1942, he joined SOE and on 11/12 August the following year, aged 43, parachuted into Indre, central France to helped run an SOE escape line from Château d'Entraygues, near Châteauroux. It is quite possible he arranged the *atterrissage*.

In an account of "*Women in Belgian History since 1830*" by Aubenas, Van Rokeghem & Vercheral-Vervoort, Madeleine was said to have worked with Louise de Lansheere, Ginette Pevtschin and Marie-Louise Hennin in the production and distribution of the clandestine newspaper *La Libre Belge*. Following the arrest and imprisonment in 1942 of the filing clerks, engravers, printers and distributors, Madeleine needed to get out of the country. The praats website, in its section on the Zero network, mentioned that she was in *Agente Connection* and in 1942 was assistant to Albert Hachez, who worked in La *Libre Belge*, and for William Ugeux, the Director-General Information and Action for State Security in London.

Frédérique Dupuich

Frédérique Dupuich's work with the Belgian State Security in London must have brought her into contact with Airey Neave, Andrée De Jongh's contact in MI9. One imagines that she would have known of the large number of women agents being trained by the SOE to be sent into France by F Section, the SOE networks supported by the British government, and RF Section, the Free French networks supported by de Gaulle. Whether she had been identified as a potential agent or whether she volunteered herself remains a mystery.

The earliest note in her personnel file was written by Lieutenant Commander Philip Johns, R.N. He gave his address as M.O.I. (S.P.), The War Office, Whitehall, S.W.1. The initials M.O.I. (S.P.) were thought by outsiders to mean the Ministry of Information Special Projects, but by those in the know as SOE HQ. Johns confirmed her interview at 11 a.m. at 'the flat' on Tuesday 12 January with Bingham. This must have been Seymour Bingham, who became head of N Section, Holland, on 1 April 1943.

Frédérique was described as 1m. 69 in height, with an oval face, normal nose, chestnut grey hair and grey green eyes. The only distinguishing feature was an appendix scar. The story she gave at her interview was that she was born on 14 February 1900 to Adolph Dupuich and Louise van Marlé in Brussels and brought up a Protestant. Fluent in French, English and Italian and knowing some German and Dutch, she attended the École Supérieure de Secrétariat in Brussels, after which she did some secretarial work and nursing. Orphaned by 1941, she said she knew Brussels, Antwerp, Gent, Flanders and Hainaut well.

Making no mention of accompanying ten Belgian soldiers and aided by Andrée De Jongh, she told them that she escaped from Brussels on 12 July 1941 by swimming the Somme canal by night. After getting to Paris she caught a train to Bayonne and crossed the border by night in the mountains near Hendaye. After being arrested in Spain and goaled at an inn she was released on the intervention of the Belgian Consular authorities. She left Spain for Tangier in Morocco and returned to Gibraltar from where she caught one of the convoy ships to England, arriving in Liverpool on 12 October 1941.

She got a job, as Connart had mentioned, working as a secretary with the Belgian State Security and in time got promoted to assistant to Captain Aronstein, the section head of the PWE and Propaganda Department. Their offices were at 38 Belgrave Square, London, S.W.1. At the time of her interview she was living at 17, Thornton Street, W.8.

Bingham decided that Frédérique was suitable for training so, after being interviewed by the SOE, she was given a commission in the FANY and sent on an 'assessment course' to determine her suitability as a radio operator at Winterfold. The report was not positive.

> *Although the candidate appeared nervous – probably through over anxiety to succeed – she worked very hard throughout the tests and showed great determination, especially in physical tests where she was unable to do very much in spite of trying very hard. She made a very good impression on the students and on the staff, and was obviously very sincere and keen to do a real job for her country. Her physical condition has not been improved through working in an office for the past two years, and though reasonably active in peace time, she is weak in the arms and having once broken her leg, - which still occasionally troubles her – it is not recommended that she be trained for parachuting. She should do very well in a liaison capacity in the field where her upbringing, appearance and manner should assist her considerably and it is in this capacity that she has been graded. She is not suitable for W/T work.*
> (TNA HS 9/40/3)

This did not stop her attending another course at S.T.S. 37.b. This was one the SOE's Special Training Schools. She was accommodated at Clobb Gorse, one of seven large country houses requisitioned by the SOE in the grounds of the Beaulieu Estate. Her weekly pay, agreed by 'T' Section, was £5, As a cover, she claimed that between 14th March and 5th August 1944 her residence was Sandwick Cottage, Estcott, Surrey.

At the end of the course, her report, dated 23rd

January 1944, indicated that Miss Dewaay, the name she had to use as a cover throughout the course, indicated that she had been given a C Plus - six out of nine for Intelligence, fail for Morse and Average for Mechanical and Instructional. It needs to be remembered that, at 44, she was one of the oldest of the women agents. Despite her age, the Station Commander commented that,

> *She is well and widely educated, is intelligent and has plenty of practical ability. She is observant and learns quickly and possesses plenty of presence of mind and has imagination.*
>
> *She is keen and worked hard, displaying good initiative. Her character is strong. She is determined, steady and reliable, but at the same time modest and unassuming.*
>
> *Her personality is pleasant; she is a good mixer with considerable charm of manner, tact and sociability. She should inspire confidence and is generally liked.*
>
> *She has good powers of leadership and should do well in any position of trust and responsibility.*
>
> <u>*CODES.*</u> *Taught Innocent Letter based on Playfair, Double transposition and Letter One-Time Pad. (Conventions fixed on all three).*
>
> *This student should prove reliable at this work. Further practice required.* (Ibid)

A week later, Hardy Amies, then Head of 'T' Section, who, like Johns, was based at M.O.I. (S.P.), queried with Lieutenant Floor of the Belgian Sûreté, whether a mission had been found for Frédérique so that additional training could be given. He intimated that she had already been on a Lysander course, practiced getting in and out in as short a time as possible and knew where to store valises and where the intercom and parachutes were. This request was passed onto 44-year-old Georges Aronstein, Captain in the reserve, who was responsible for making the arrangements for the dropping of PWE agents into Belgium and France.

On 8 March, in a letter marked SECRET, Aronstein wrote to Major Deacon of the Propaganda Information Department at Bush House, Aldwych, London, W.C. 2. in which we learn of Frédérique's code name.

> *Dear Deacon,*
> <u>*CONSTANTIN*</u>
> *I have now had the opportunity to see S.O.E. Syllabus of propaganda courses given at S.T.S. 39.* [Wall Hall, Aldenham, Hertfordshire]
> *It strikes me that one of the outside courses, the last one, c) on page 4, should be of great interest to Constantin. Is it possible to lay it on?*
> *Constantin expressed the desire to have before his departure a personal knowledge of some striking features, for instance, an important sitting of the House of Commons; a bomber command station at the departure of the planes; a B.B.C. visit with a broadcasting of news.*
> *Would you kindly let me know whether you could arrange these or other visits?*
> *Yours sincerely,*
> *Capitaine Aronstein* (Ibid)

To add weight, an almost identical request was made to Amies by Flight Lieutenant P.H. *Hamilton Mack* whose response was that she ought not to get the additional training until it was certain she was going. On 14 March he wrote:

> *My dear Deacon,*
> <u>*Constantin*</u>
> *I have the pleasure to inform you that it is more than likely that we shall have a place on a Lysander for the above Agent during the April Moon. I hope to have definite news within the next 3 or 4 days. As you know, however, these things are on the lap of the gods.*
> <u>*In the circumstances, it is imperative that she be ready and fully briefed by March 28th.*</u>

> *You will see, therefore, that it is impossible to give her the additional background training that you have suggested, if we are to seize this opportunity of dispatching her by Lysander – an opportunity which, I am sure you will agree, it would be folly to reject, knowing, as you do, how difficult these places are to obtain.*
> *Yours ever,* (Ibid)

The French Section agreed that she could take a seat on their planned flight to France in the moon period at the beginning of April. Presumably the drop zone was in northern France as Deacon was told on 18 March in an unsigned letter, presumably from Amies.

> *As regards her movements from France to Belgium we can help her and full instructions will be included in her operation order. It will however be necessary for you to supply details of her contacts.*
> *I presume that she will establish herself and then make contact with HECTOR or SOCRATES but I leave these details of course to you. In due course I think we should warn HECTOR of her arrival and I should also like to inform VERGILIA for his information.*
> *Yours ever,* (Ibid)

Analysis of the SOE missions listed on the Adam Matthews Publications website showed that Hector was a name that appeared in the outlines of many SOE missions to Belgium. The HILLCAT mission in August 1943 involved sending André Wendelen, codenamed Tybalt, to work as a radio operator for Hector. When his friend Burgers was captured, the SCIPION mission was planned for Philippe de Liedekerke to replace him. In January 1944, with a field name Iago, he was parachuted in to provide Wendelen with support for a counter-scorch organisation in Antwerp and to investigate the security of the Hector group following the recent arrests. In the same month François Flour was sent on operation HORATIO to

Brussels to be the radio operator for Hector II and Nelly. Glove was arrested in May 1944. In March 1944 the MONTANO mission dropped Henri Neumann, a Comète evader, to report on Group G activities, to investigate the Yapok, Fabius and Hector II missions and create the P.W.E structure and sabotage activities in central Brussels. Their stories are told by Foot in *The SOE in the Low Countries.*

SOCRATES was a mission established in 1943 to organise financial aid to resistance organizations in Belgium. It was run by Major Raymond Scheyven, a Doctor of Law and director of the Allard Bank. 'He had built up a nation-wide organisation for the distribution of funds to the many Resistance groups operating under the control of SOE.' Partly funded from Britain, Scheyven received considerable financial help from patriotic industrialists and bankers inside Belgium. (Johns, op.cit.p.158) Dirk Luyten, a researcher at CEGESOMA in Brussels, commented that

> *E. Verhoeyen researched the sometimes difficult relation between the resistance movements and the British Intelligence Services and the government in London. He looked at a number of missions of secret agents and mapped the support of the service Socrates for forced labourers. This network took, in the name of the government in exile in London, loans from industrialists and bankers to support persons in hiding.* (http://www.cegesoma.be/docs/media/Bibliographies/Bibliography_ESF.pdf 25th June 2009)

A search of the online catalogue Pallas at CEGESOMA revealed that VEIGILIA CNC was number 163 for SOE Belgium. An Internet search revealed nothing but Connart told me that Virgilia was Joseph Guillery, alias Nelly. He had been landed by Lysander in France to co-ordinate all the resistance movements in France. The results were slow and ineffective so Idesbald Floor and Georges Marchand were parachuted in on

11/12 April 1944 to assess the problem. Floor reported in May that that the Resistance was divided. The dbnl website had more information on VIRGILIA. A translation of their website reads:

> *Respectively in July and August 1943 Philippe de Liedekerke (Claudius) and Andre Wendelen (Tybalt, Hector) were sent to Belgium with the mandate to liaise with the OR in helping to organize work objectors. It created the service Socrates, led by R. Scheyven. 'Socrates' built in part on some earlier PWE items, because Harnisfeger (Dingo, parachuted in November 1942) was already at the regional level, in the region of Charleroi, qualified workers managed to escape the compulsory employment. Contact with the BNB was made. This first contact, which PWE, SOE and the SV administered, led to a rather complex set of items to the 'civil' resistance and finally culminated in the establishment of a National Coordination Committee. It was made up of representatives of the Secret Army, Group G, the BNB and the Partisans OR. The operation of this Committee was led by Jules Guillery (Nelly, Virgilia) and Jules Rolin, later by Lepoivre (July 1944).* (http://www.dbnl.org/tekst/vijv003belg01_01/vijv003belg01_01_0008.htm 25th June 2009)

Connart mentioned that Frédérique had been a much appreciated assistant at PWE. Sefton Delmer, a Berlin-born Daily Express correspondent who, with the blessing of Winston Churchill, created PWE in September 1941. It was a right-wing organisation which generated white, grey and black propaganda, which was then disseminated into occupied Europe. White would be true and its source acknowledged. Black would be false and attributed to others. Grey was a mix.

Maybe Frédérique was involved amongst many ancillary tasks in the Belgian Section, in preparing radio messages to be broadcast by the BBC or on fake German radio stations. She was involved with planning newspapers and brochures that were dropped over Belgium by the Special Duties Squadrons.

It appears that the plan was for Frédérique to work alongside these groups prior to D-Day. On 21 March 1944 Hamilton Mack wrote the following letter to Amies in which, intriguingly, all the instances of she and her were changed to he and him or his.

> MOST SECRET
> Dear Amies,
> DEWAAY
> I have to acknowledge the receipt of your letter ref HA/993, dated 18.3.44, of the above heading.
> I am pleased to see that there are very good possibilities of this Agent being included in a Lysander operation, and having discussed the matter with Aronstein, we both agree that we should avail ourselves of the means offered.
> Aronstein is most certainly "getting on with her mission" and it has in fact been arranged that she should be seen on Friday next, 24th inst., in order to be briefed and for details of her contacts to be supplied.
> After arrival, she will contact Hector II who will put her in touch with Socrates. Would you be kind enough, in due course, to warn Hector of her arrival and presumably you will take such steps as you consider necessary as far as Vergilia is concerned.
> Yours sincerely, (TNA HS 9/460/3)

The planned mission for the *"coming moon to take up Mademoiselle Dewaay and some of the stores asked for by Greyhound for Woodchuck 2"*, SOE agents already in the field, did not go ahead. The reason Amies told Floor on 21 March *was a technicality.*

> *"…It was our intention to try and lay on a Lysander operation with the above circuit for this I have received the following communication*

from our Air Ministry liaison: - 'I would call your attention to the ruling laid down by the Air Ministry than men in the field who have not successfully completed the courses in this country have no authority either to lay the flarepath for landing operations, or to be responsible for carrying out these operations in other respects. It is essential to stick to the ruling that the man whose name is submitted – provided he has successfully completed a course – lays on the operation, and that he is present in person. I therefore regret that we are unable to lay on this operation this moon'
    This means that the operation is off but as you know we have managed to get Dewaay up on a French operation." (Ibid.)

The documents stated that all the arrangements had been made to get her from France into Belgium and, once in place, to be supplied with containers courtesy of 138 Squadron.

29 March
MISSION CONSTANTIN (Mlle DUPUY, DEWAAY)
In despatches of containers to the field destined ultimately either for HECTOR or SOCRATES, will you please enclose a regular grocery supplies for CONSTANTIN. This should include: tea, sugar, chocolate, soap, cigarettes and, if possible, whisky.
(Ibid.)

In reality, communications in that part of France were broken. Bridges had been blown up, railways sabotaged and roads were being daily strafed by planes. Frédérique was to be dropped with Gérard II, her radio operator, who her notes stated "*had also to contact Joséphine, who, as you know, is in a position to procure locally enlisted W/T's.*" She had messages to take, copies of which were in her file:

POUR HECTOR
<u>W/T Operators</u>

Two operators, SHOELACE and KELLING, are now in the field.
We are surprised by SHOELACE's long silence and worried with regard to his frequencies; we count on you to take this matter in hand.
SHOELACE in principle affects your service, but you may, if you judge it opportune, transmit the messages of our other missions by your intermediary, provided it's agreed.
Regarding KELLING, in principal he deals with the needs of SOCRATES and CONSTANTIN. However, if he isn't involved exclusively in these concerns, because we always liaise with, you can use him to transmit other messages if you think fit. Please give equal priority to accommodation, supplies, surveillance groups and the other various mission tasks.
B. Shipments
We hope to achieve monthly shipments of sixty containers destined for your PWE missions. These shipments will be about fifteen containers per drop; thus you need to find four dropping zones each moon.
We believe that MANDRILL III is able to receive fifteen containers each month. He wanted us to indicate a drop zone for your intermediary. There are another forty-five containers which will contain the "Manual" which FABIUS had already trained you in. Their distribution will be assured as follows:
For the Deux Flandres by the care of FABIUS
For the rest of Belgium, by the care of the other missions and according to your instructions.
C, Couriers received via Shrew
It is under control and we are concerned with this lack. It contains, on first sight, information, suggestions and extremely sensitive information, which will be the object of deep study. We will get back to you shortly. In the meantime we really thank you for the marvellous work that you have done.

We have also received many of your requests for a Swiss courier; however we ask that you use your previous code.
D. The General Situation
The situation regarding our PWE missions is confused. It is essential that we have their detailed reports as soon as possible; let us get a Swiss courier, in your code or by other interesting missions. (Ibid.)

SHOELACE, according to Connart, was a British agent, Henri D[?], alias *Yapock, Dark* and *Lainbert*. He had been parachuted into Belgium on 8 February 1944 with Henri Neuman and Émile Van Dyck as a replacement for Wittold Lobet. His name does not appear in Strubbe's book. Following his arrest he was said to have broken under questioning and 'collaborated'. After liberation, it was proposed that he should stand trial in England but instead ordered to undertake a hazardous Intelligence mission, parachuting onto an island in the Pacific, where the Japanese were refusing to capitulate. By the time he arrived, they had already surrendered.

Frédérique was given a large amount of money to take. A note Floor wrote to Amies said that Captain Ferry had agreed that 110,000 Belgian francs could be taken from funds Amies controlled for the LENA and VARRIUS mission. Amies added in pencil: *"extracted from Othello II package."* I found no references to Varrius but VARRO was an SOE mission to Belgium in 1944. Georges Marchand, field name, *Delphine* was parachuted in to investigate the arrests in the Tybalt organisation.

It seems very likely that the arrests mentioned above explained Hamilton Mack's brief note in her file dated 8th April that *"Dadson and I attended a meeting with Sûrete this morning, when it was decided that Constantin's departure would be deferred until certain development had taken place. I think Ugeux notified Johns, but as I am unable to get either of you on the phone this afternoon in order to confirm the foregoing, it may be useful to place the decision on record."* Mr. Ugeux, was the Director-

General 'Information and Action for State Security in London.' An undated note stated that *"LENA Mission now definitely cancelled."* which prompted Deacon to ask that her additional training be provided.

By the beginning of May, things started to look more optimistic for Frédérique's mission. Amies wrote to Floor:

> 5th May
> *As regards LENA, the operation order is being altered to give effect to the decision that KELLING is intended to act as W/T operator to LENA and likewise to ensure the W/T communications to SOCRATES.*
>
> *The only points which arose in connection with the LENA mission as such were: firstly, that it is desirable to emphasise that there should be no contact between LENA and NELLY except through SOCRATES: and secondly, that contact with Group G, should only be through NELLY via SOCRATES.*
>
> *The suggestion made in the mission that LENA should apply to NELLY for a direct with Group G. is not acceptable.*
>
> *… Much the best solution from our point of view would be that all solidarity payments to the dependents of Active group members should be made by our own liaison officers from funds drawn direct from us, or raised by the liaison officers in the field in agreement with Service Action here; and that LENA should not intervene at all in payments to the "Active" groups, vis. F.I.L., Sabotage and Partisans; Group G. It is suggested that LENA should not be allowed to use KELLING for W/T communications. The proposed solution is that the W/T traffic of SOCRATES and LENA should be assured through the SAMOYEDE operator.* (Ibid)

According to the Adams Matthews Publications website, SAMOYEDE was sent out in May 1943 as a Political Intelligence Department mission for pre- and post- liberation work, the jamming of German wireless installations and helping the Allies from D-Day in the use of press, cinema and radio.

In a note dated 27 May 1944 headed Agent LENA, it stated that permission had been granted for Frédérique to proceed to the Field, via France, by Lysander operation on 30 May. Almost certainly aware of the Allies impending plans for the following week, Floor sent Amies the following:

> *27th May*
>
> *Please find enclosed herewith two notes to be taken by CONSTANTIN in micro-photo farm to SOCRATES. Also one original of an introduction note for Mr. Lucien Fuss which should be camouflaged in Constantin's luggage.*
>
> *She should be reminded before leaving that Mr. Lucien Fuss, Director of the "Soir", 76, Rue St. Bernard, 3eme étage, can be contacted towards 11 a.m. this will enable her to be put into contact with Mr. Henri Fuss.*
>
> *LENA*
> *AGNES A SOCRATES*
> *1. Pleased to know you.*
> *2. Felicitations on work well done.*
> *3. The emissary promises that the pianist (radio operator) will be with you soon.*
> *4. Help all your friends without exception.*
> *5. Hope it goes well. Good Luck. Cheerio.*
>
> *LENA*
> *AGNES A TUNIS*
> *1. Happy to have this occasion to make your acquaintance.*
> *2. Thanks for your services.*
> *3. Worried no news about promised passengers.*
> *4. Complete approval to burn any ciphers which trouble your conscience.*
> *5. God Bless you. Cheerio. (Ibid.)*

These seem to have been key commands to the various resistance groups to commence their planned activities to coincide with D-Day. Further notes were sent for her to take including an introductory note from Mr Lepage to Mr Jean de Landsheere, which Amies was asked to hide in Constantin's luggage and fifteen treasure bills to be given to Socrates. However, the flight did not go ahead. Amies explained why to Floor two days after D-Day.

> *8th June 1944*
> *Dear Ides*
> *CONSTANTIN*
> *With reference to your letter of 7th June, as you know, the above operation was put on at least three times during the past 8 days but was cancelled at the last minute owing to weather. It has now been postponed indefinitely owing to recent events, and it is not considered in any way feasible to send a Lysander (which is an almost unarmed aircraft and slow flying) over France.*
> *As you are aware, we are entirely dependent on the goodwill of the French section in this matter and you can be certain that they were as anxious to get the operation off as we were, as they were not only sending at least one of their agents on the same aircraft, but also wanted to pick up some as well.*
> *It is extremely unfortunate for poor CONSTANTIN, but I must point out that we have all along said that this operation would not go off, although very definite hopes were raised again when the French section offer the seat at the beginning of the last moon.*
> *Yours ever,* (Ibid.)

Presumably, the important messages were sent in code to a radio operator in the field and those from Agnès sent as part of the BBC's *"messages personnels"* after the 1900 hours news. One wonders what was going through

Frédérique's mind with all the planning and preparation, expectations being raised and then dashed. One imagines that she was still in London and in receipt of her £5 a week. A month after D-Day, Captain Aronstein noted Amies with a copy to Mr. Ugeux,

> 6th July
> CONSTANTIN
> If this agent seems unfortunately not to have a chance to leave this moon period, she has asked me to inform you that she decides to go on the SOE mission
> Having agreed a regular engagement in the FANY she asks to be regularly incorporated into this organisation and to know what affectations need to be given?
> CONSTANTIN asks that a precise answer be given within eight days. (Ibid)

The reply a few days later informed Aronstein that Constantin had been engaged in the FANY Special Section, which permitted women agents to wear uniform during their training and carry a weapon. If this training was, for one reason or another, terminated, the agent automatically had to return to civilian life unless special means were taken to employ her in the active side of the FANYs.

An insight into what she must have gone through was provided in the personnel file of Anne-Marie Walters, one of the women agents sent into France. When she returned to England after the war, she was interviewed by a reporter working for the BBC following a government announcement about women being sent as spies into France. Whether it was forced by the media discovering that women had been sent into occupied Europe, one does not know but both the *Daily Express* and *Daily Telegraph* ran articles on female spies. What follows is the transcript of the interview in March 1945 that had to be sent to SOE for vetting. The text in bold had to be deleted before the programme was allowed to transmit it.

CUE MATERIAL FOR PARACHUTE GIRL

On March 5th, Sir Archibald Sinclair revealed for the first time in his speech to the Commons that members of the Women's Auxiliary Air Force have been to the fore in helping the Resistance groups in Europe before the landing on D-Day, either as Liaison officers, or couriers or radio operators.
We have in the studio today a girl who was parachuted into France many months before D-Day (and) *remained several months after fighting with the Maquis. This WAAF had an English father and a French mother and was brought up in Geneva and she begins this interview with Vera Lindsay by telling how she was chosen for this special work.*

LINDSAY: Tell me – how was it you were chosen to be parachuted into France to do this special work?
PARA.GIRL: Well you see I was born and brought up in Geneva and my mother is French, so that I actually speak French much better than English. And what is more, consider that France is my country really from a patriotic point of view.
LINDSAY: Tell me – you came to England when, exactly?
PARA.GIRL: I came in 1940 just after the S…. had happened and I had actually never come to England before that.
LINDSAY: And what did you start doing? How did they find you?
PARA.GIRL: Well I was in the WAAFs and as I'd always made quite a lot of noise about being able to speak French and wanted to do some work having to do with the Free French and I had been on the list for transfer of jobs for some time.
LINDSAY: Tell me – how long did you train for this special work and was the training very difficult?
PARA.GIRL: Well I trained quite a long time, and the training was extremely interesting and very useful to

me but I'm afraid I cannot talk at all about that right now.
LINDSAY: Were there other women training with you?
PARA.GIRL: Yes, there were a number of other women training with me. Quite a number trained after I left and went later too,
LINDSAY: But were they English girls who spoke French?
PARA.GIRL: Some were French but most of them were English girls speaking absolutely fluent French. Actually French like a native woman.
LINDSAY: Now tell me, I know I can't ask you questions but tell me this – what is it like just before when you know already that you were – you had finished your training and were leaving for France? What were the days like just before that?
PARA.GIRL: Well to be quite honest they were rather nerve-racking, because we were supposed to leave in November 1943 but the weather was so bad, flying conditions were so poor that there was no question of leaving until the beginning of January. Every morning we'd call at our office at eleven o'clock and they invariably answered that the weather was too bad for that same night, but that we had to go on standing by and we just studied maps and studied the conditions of life in the particular region we were going to, and tried to get as much information as we could from this end of the work.
LINDSAY: But what about the region you were going to? Did you know it at all?
PARA.GIRL: No, I didn't know it at all and as a matter of fact it was particularly chosen so that I shouldn't. So that I should not run the risk of falling into people who had seen me going and leaving France and who knew that I hadn't been in France the last years and who obviously would immediately guess how I had arrived and what I

was doing.
LINDSAY: *But in those days just before you left were you able to see ordinary people? I mean your friends in London?*
PARA.GIRL: *Well the only people I knew and frequented so to speak were my friends who were doing the same job as I was and my family didn't know anything about it and we had worked out all our stories to the last details. Whenever they came at home they never mentioned anything of the work we were doing. My parents knew I was doing secret work but they didn't know at all, they didn't have any idea what it was. And my friends played up to the game very well.*

LINDSAY: And tell me, how are you dressed for this, for this dropping from the sky into France?
PARA.GIRL: I was dressed exactly as I am now walking around in the streets of London. I had a tweed suit on and a fur coat and I had some a jump suit on top of course – but the idea was that I should be just one of the crowd of people in France as soon as I arrived there.

LINDSAY: *And just before the jump – what was the feeling? Were you afraid?*
PARA.GIRL: *No, I wasn't afraid. In fact it was the only time in all the jumps that I have made that I really wasn't afraid at all. There were so many things to think about and it was our second trip. The pilot had circled some time in the region before being able to contact our people on the ground and we had a horrible moment that we should have to go back once more. And when the pilot declared that he had contacted the people and we were to go to action stations and jump – I felt so relieved at the idea that we wouldn't have to go back again to England it was really quite a pleasure.*

LINDSAY: And tell me – did you feel very much in danger from the moment you landed?
PARA.GIRL: Well at first I did – I felt very obvious – I had a feeling that I was so obvious as I would

have been if I had been walking on the maps that I had been studying all that time just before leaving – but that's a feeling that soon left me and I was very easily – very easy to disappear in the crowd.
LINDSAY: Where did you live during the time that you were there?
PARA.GIRL: I lived in a farm the whole time. The farmers acted like parents to me. They never even asked me for a single centime in repayment for all they were doing for me. And they looked after me and helped me and the whole time and they weren't even worried about me – about themselves actually.
LINDSAY: Did they know what you were doing?
PARA.GIRL: Yes they did – of course it's too much to ask of anybody to be doing a thing like that without knowing what dangers they were risking.
LINDSAY: Yes but how did they – what did they say to the neighbours – I means how did they explain your arrival?
PARA.GIRL: Well everybody said that I was a student from Paris who just couldn't go on with her studies because life in Paris was so expensive and so different and who had come to seek refuge with the farmer who was supposed to be a friend of my father in the last war. That story took very well. It was very simple and normal there and everybody around the farm believed it and I should think they still believe it to this day. (TNA HS 9/339/2)

One guesses that Frédérique/Constantin/Lena's mission had not changed when she was eventually landed in central France on 6th August. There were no details in her file about it, nor any debriefing notes. The last document was a note dated 11 August saying that Floor sent Captain Peter Ferry to Amies with 32,000 US dollar bills *"in balance of CONSTANTIN operational funds."*

Connart told me that on 6 August, 44-year-old Frédérique was flown in a light plane, thought to have been a Lysander, to France. Examination of 138 and 161 Squadron records do not mention specifically the dropping a female agent. Thomas Ensminger, the Carpetbagger's historian, told me that there were no flights from RAF Harrington on 3/4th August. However, there had been a double drop mission to Belgium on the night of 4/5 August but the operational records were not clear where the three 'Joes' were dropped. The Liberator dropped them blind, not to a designated drop zone, one which they would have to have made their own way from without the help of a reception committee. The mission names were *Tybalt 15* and *Flavius 18*. Tybalt was André Wendelen's code name. Connart thought that Flavius was probably a typo for Claudius, de Liedekerke's code name.

Freddie Clark, one of the Tempsford pilots, identified in his *"Agents by Moonlight,"* two Halifax missions on 5/6th August. Only one went to Belgium. 161 Squadron Records showed that the pilot F/L Green took off at 2215 hours and reached his second target, mission SOUBRETTE, at 0124 hours mission dropping three agents, eleven containers and three packages. Being secret missions there is no wonder that there is little evidence of these drops.

Once she landed near Genillé in Indre-et-Loire, she was taken to a small hotel in Saint-Jean near Loches. *"Romain"*, the chief of the local reception committee, sent a scout to Tours where he learned that the Gestapo had arrested her planned contacts on 25 July.

No wonder her mission had been delayed. The whole transport system was in chaos. The roads were being continuously machine-gunned, trains were non-existent and telephone and telegraph wires had been cut. It was only a month after D-Day. In July 1944, an estimated 800 demolitions had been undertaken, more than forty trains derailed and more than sixty bridges destroyed. (Johns, P. *Within Two Cloaks: Missions with SIS and SOE,* William Kimber, (1979), p.137)

With no means of contacting London, Frédérique

bought a bike for 8,000 French francs but learned that ishe was rapidly becoming known in the area as a "British parachutist." The area she was working in had changed hands three times. She spent weeks trying to get contacts in a region where the Germans were harassing the French Maquis. She was captured and imprisoned three times by both the French resistance and the French authorities but managed to survive their interrogations and, according to Connart, the obvious desire of the authorities to lynch her. The first time was at Bois de Verneuil when the local resistance released her after checking at Genillé. A few hours later she was arrested by the French 2e Bureau and sent to the concentration camp at Pressigny-le-Grand alongside German POWs, French traitors and prostitutes.

Bouvier, the French commandant and military Chief of Staff, only released her on Sunday 10 September 1944. She reached Tours by bicycle where she met an American officer and, after a long and hazardous midnight drive in a jeep, arrived at the US 9th Army headquarters in Rennes, Brittany. Two hours after registering at a hotel, she was arrested again, this time by the French Police who held her at 63 Boulevard de Sevigne, a building used to question suspected 'terrorists'. Once she succeeded in getting released on 16 September, she regained contact with the Americans who she convinced to fly her to Paris. Five days later, Major Benn of the SIS, allowed her to return to Brussels. Her attitude, if not her mission, was considered very valuable. When she arrived back in England in October,

> She next volunteered for special duties in South East Asia and after taking the Oath of Allegiance at Chicheley Hall, Buckinghamshire (one of SOE's training schools), *she left for India on April 15th 1945. Various duties in formerly Japanese occupied territory, Sumatra, Java etc., kept her in the S.E.A.C. area until she left for England in June 1946, where she was demobilised.* (TNA HO 405/10578)

She worked for a while as a librarian in the British Embassy in Brussels and successfully applied for British naturalisation, eventually settling on the south coast of England. Her file in the Belgium MoD *Ondersectie Notariaat Archieven* stated that during her time working for State Security in London:

> "*With ardour and tenacity she devoted herself totally to the intelligence service in its fight against the enemy. Compromised by her activities, she escaped Belgium and spontaneously offered to undertake a perilous mission in occupied territory. She gave a magnificent example of unselfish patriotism.*" (HRG-A/N-Archives 3258664)

Her exploits earned her the King's Medal for Courage, which was presented to her at the War Office by General Montgomery, the Croix de Guerre avec Palme, the Chevalier de l'ordre de Léopold III for exceptional service rendered to her country, the Croix des Evades, the Resistance Medal, the General Service Medal with clasp and the France and Germany campaign medals. (National Archives HS 9/460/3)

On 2 September 1944, the Allies crossed into Belgium. On hearing the news 1,760 prisoners and sixty-three Allied airmen were taken from St Gilles prison and put on trains for Germany. Sabotage and negotiation stopped the train before the border and the men released the following day. On that day, 3 September, the U.S. First Army took Tournai and the following day the British Second Army and a Belgian group liberated Brussels. Although their aim was to cross the Rhine, the port of Antwerp had to be taken first to secure the supplies for the British, Canadian and American armies. The British 11th Armoured Division took the city on the 4 September and, thanks to the work of Group G, without the docks being damaged and the energy companies destroyed. The sixty miles (96 kms.) of the Scheldt estuary had then to be cleared by the Canadians, a long and difficult task.

Ghent was reached by the 5 September and the British entered Liège on the 6th. The Canadians had surrounded Calais, trapping the German garrison whilst the Americans pushed east, crossing the Meuse to liberate Ghent and Courtrai. The British 11th Armoured Division crossed the Albert Canal, east of Antwerp, on the 7 September. On the following day the Canadians took Ostend and the Americans took control of Liège and the first Allied troops entered Germany, near Aachen on the 10 September. After fifty-nine months of occupation, Belgium was liberated.

However, according to a report from Moscow to Sir A. Clark Kerr, there were concerns about what appeared to have been reaction to a Communist demonstration.

Following is extract from MOSCOW News of November 29th.

"What is happening in Belgium today cannot but give cause for uneasiness among those who are fighting Hitlerite Germany and all those who sincerely want to see Europe free from Fascism and Fascist influence.

Belgium has just been redeemed. Frightful period of German Fascist domination is still fresh in everyone's memory. Belgium people hve not yet had time to straighten their backs or taste the sweetness of freedom to the full. Front is still close by. But already the blood of Belgiuan patriots has been spilt on the streets of BRUSSELS.

Who were demonstrators at whom police fired? Were any criminals? Fascists? Fifth Column perhaps. No they were men and women who, working deep in underground, prepared for the hour when they could strike at Germans, men nd women who did not submit to the enemy, people whose conscience is not weighed down by 'collaboration' with Hitlerites. They were people who in the face of Hitlerite terror, raised the banner of implacable struggle against German invaders. Now Belgian

Gendarmes shot them down. One can imagine how welcome the news must have been in BERLIN, how gleefully Hitlerite bandits rubbed their hands

Events in Belgium and behaviour of authorities have evoked indignation among all freedom loving peoples. Belgian Government has commenced its activity by supressing the very forces that were instrumental in bringing it back to Belgium. Whoe interests does this campaign against internal forces of resistance serve? Only the interests of Fifth Column interests of those who collaborated with the Germans. STEELE, American radio commentator, threw light on Belgian events when he said they may be called political counter offensive of cartels. For the past twenty years Belgian Governments have for the most part been only puppets of Societe General de Belgique, an interesting syndicate controlling all Belgian industrial enterprises and banks in its colonies, he said, pointing out that PIERLOT Government is no exception and tht it evidently believes its mission to be restoration of status quo which means saving Belgian industrialists who collaborated with the Germans.

It goes without saying that country freed from Hitlerite oppression must have order. But primary task of establishing order is not to crush anti-Fascist forces, but to wipe out remnants of Fifth Column, remnants of Hitlerite influence. He who ids Hitlerite agencies and helps to preserve "new order" after withdrawal of Germans aids Hitlerite bandits in commission of their crimes and not the just and righteous cause of the United Nations. That is why the shooting in BRUSSELS alarms all those who stand for the real struggle gainst Hitlerism.., that deadly peril to mankind, to rid the world of which freedom loving nations have sacrificed and are still sacrificing so much. (TNA HS7/227)

One imagines that the anonymous blonde played her part in the war effort but Frédérique, Elaine and Olga undertook vital missions in the last few weeks of the Belgium occupation. This account has revealed, perhaps for the first time, some of the behind-the-scenes activity that led to these four extremely brave women returning to the field. They must have known the Allies were about to invade and felt that they could play the part planned for them in forcing the enemy out and liberating their country.

Bibliography and Suggested Reading

Aubenas, J. Van Rokeghem, S. & Vercheral-Vervoort, J. (2006), Des femmes dans l'histoire de Belgique, depuis 1830, Editions Luc Pire
Bailey, Roderick, *The Independent*, Andrée De Jongh: Organiser of the Comet line, Thursday, 6 December 2007
Clark, F. (1999), *Agents by Moonlight – The Secret History of RAF Tempsford during the Second World War*, Tempus Publishing Ltd., Stroud
Crowdy, T. (2008), *SOE Agent: Churchill's Secret Warriors*, Osprey Publishing
Elliot, S. and Fox, J. (2009), *The Children who Fought Hitler,* John Murray
Foot, M.R.D. (2001), *SOE in the Low Countries*, St. Ermin's press
Dujardin, V. & and van den Wijngaert, M. (2001), *Léopold III,*
Neave, A. (1954), *Little Cyclone,* Hodder and Stoughton
Neave, A. (1969), *Saturday at MI9,* Hodder and Staughton
O'Connor, B. (2009), *Return to Holland,* private publication
Remy, Adeline, (2007). 'L'engagement des femmes dans la ligne d'évasion Comète(1941-1944): entre mythe et réalité?', in *Femmes et résistance en Belgique et en zone interdite : 1940-1944*. Colloque organisé à Bondues par l'institut de recherches historiques du septentrion, IRHIS, et la ville de Bondues le 28 janvier 2006, Villeneuve d'Ascq : Université Charles-de-Gaulle-Lille 3, IRHIS. Institut de recherches historiques du septentrion, pp.57-72
Remy, Adeline & Debruyne, Emmanuel, (2009), 'Le financement des services de renseignements et des lignes d'évasion belges', in : *La clandestinité en Belgique et en zone interdite (1940-1944)*. Colloque organisé à Bondues par l'institut de recherches historiques du septentrion, IRHIS, et la ville de Bondues le 28 janvier 2008, Villeneuve d'Ascq : Université Charles-de-Gaulle-Lille 3, IRHIS. Institut de recherches historiques du septentrion.
Richards, Lee, *Black Art: British Clandestine Psychological Warfare against the Third Reich,* www.pyswar.org, 2010
Strubbe, F. (1998) *Services Secrets Belges 1940 – 1945,*

Gand, Madoc
Wheeler, S. Interview with Andrée De Jongh published in *Bulletin* 2000
Thompson, G.T.R. (Major), (1963), *NOTES ON S.O.E. 1941 to 1943 with special reference to The Belgian Country Section*

Documents in the National Archives:
FO 898/90, PWE Emilia mission file
FO 898/94, PWE Missions in Belgium: Agents, activities, reports, messages and correspondence.
HS 6/84 Olga Jackson,
HS 6/112 Elaine Madden
HS 6/142, Porcupine – Mandrill mission report
HS 9/460/3 Frédérique Dupuich
HO 405/10578 Frédérique Dupuich
HS 6/216 Patron Lysander
HS 6/44 Andre Wendelen
HS 7/227 Survey of Global Activities 1-15 February 1942
HS 9/339/2 Anne-Marie Walters

Documents held by CEGESOMA, Belgium
Dossier Archives Notariales Défense 003.269.945

Ondersectie Notariaat Archieven, Brussels
HRG-A/N-Archives
3258664
2363363 Madden

Websites
http://www.1914-1918.be/civil_walthere_dewe.php
http://www.91stbombgroup.com/91st_info/schweinfurt_raid.html
http://www.archives@mundaneum.be
http://www.belgiansas.com/history.html
http://www.belgiumww2.info
http://www.christopherlong.co.uk/pub/rafes.html
http://home.clara.net/clinchy/bulletin.htm

http://home.clara.net/clinchy/cometeph.htm
http://www.comete-bidassoa.com/fr_1943.htm
http://www.comteline.org/ficheB003.html
http://www.cometeline.org/ABChelpers.html#GoffinetBaron
http://www.cometeline.org/cometaviateurpasse.html
http://www.conscript-heroes.com/escapelines/EscapeLines.html
http://www.dailymail.co.uk/news/article-1222375/The-children-fought-Hitler-How-British-expats-Third-Reichs-fiercest-foes.html
http://www.dbnl.org/tekst/vijv003belg01_01/vijv003belg01_01_0008.htm
http://educationforum.ipbhost.com/index.php?showtopic=11545
http://www.express.co.uk/posts/view/136095/The-children-who-fought-Hitler-
http://www.guardian.co.uk/news/2007/oct/22/guardianobituaries.obituaries
http://www.praats.be/clarence.htm
http://www.praats.be/zero.htm
http://users.skynet.be/bs281548/comethist.htm
http://www.spartacus.schoolnet.co.uk/FRjongh.htm
http://www.telegraph.co.uk/news/obituaries/1566506/Andrée-de-Jongh.html
http://www.telegraph.co.uk/news/obituaries/1349750/Peggy-Langley.html
http://www.theroyalforums.com/forums/f159/prince-charles-count-of-flanders-1903-1983-a-13809.html
http://www.thompsononename.org.uk
http://www.timesonline.co.uk/tol/comment/obituaries/article2657876.ece
http://www.truenorthperspective.com/24104.jpg
http://www.verzetsmuseum.org
http://www.west-vlaanderen.be/NL/Leefomgeving/raversijde/welcome/thememorialprinceKarel/Pages/PrinceKarel.aspx
http://en.wikipedia.org/wiki/Andrée_de_Jongh

TV Documentary
The Children who Fought Hitler, Testimony Films, shown on BBC 4, 8 November 2009

Return to Belgium

www.ingramcontent.com/pod-product-compliance
Lightning Source LLC
LaVergne TN
LVHW051636080426
835511LV00016B/2360